Colonial Forts of South Carolina 1670-1775

Larry E. Ivers

TRICENTENNIAL BOOKLET NUMBER 3

Published for the South Carolina Tricentennial Commission
by the University of South Carolina Press
Columbia, South Carolina

First Edition

Copyright © 1970 by
The University of South Carolina Press

Published in Columbia, S. C., by
The University of South Carolina Press, 1970

Standard Book Number: 87249-135-8

Library of Congress Catalog Card Number: 71-113805

Manufactured in the United States of America
By Vogue Press, Inc.

Contents

South Carolina's Colonial Frontier 1
A Description of the Forts and their Garrisons . . . 24
A List of the Principal Forts 37

Illustrations

South Carolina Forts, 1670–1699 2
South Carolina Defenses, 1700–1714 4
Yamassee War Forts, 1715–1716 8
South Carolina Forts, 1717–1735 13
South Carolina Forts, 1736–1759 15
Cherokee War Forts, 1760–1761 19
South Carolina Forts, 1762–1775 22
Fort Johnson, 1711 25
A Plantation Fort 27
Fort Moore, 1724 29
Charles Town's Fortifications, 1695–1745 41
Congaree Fort (old fort), 1718–1722 44
Fort King George, 1721–1727 53
Fort Loudoun, 1756–1760 59
Fort Lyttelton, 1758–1775 61
Fort Prince Frederick, 1731–1758 68
Fort Prince George (Keowee), 1753–1768 71

South Carolina's Colonial Frontier

Charles Town was fortified against possible attack by Spaniards and Indians in 1670, the first year of its settlement. The village was protected by a moat and a fence of logs called a palisade. Fortunately, the Indians living along the coast, a Muskhogean division named Cusabo, were friendly to the South Carolinians. Other tribes in the interior posed more problems. Southeastern North America was the home of several large Indian Nations, many of whom were then on the rise to power. The Creeks, Cherokees, Yamassees, Chickasaws, and Choctaws were the most numerous. Other small tribes, the Shawnees, Yuchis, Catawbas, Westoes, and others, also had to be reckoned with because of their extreme warlike nature.

The Westoes, living near present Augusta, Georgia, were often troublesome. Most of the exposed plantations, notably St. Giles and Mepkin, were fortified against their depredations. Outbreaks occurred in 1673, and during the years 1680-1683 South Carolina practically exterminated the Westoes through the use of the Savannahs, a tribe of wandering Shawnee Indians who had arrived from present Tennessee and allied themselves with the South Carolinians. Thus, the settlers learned quite early that the best method of defense

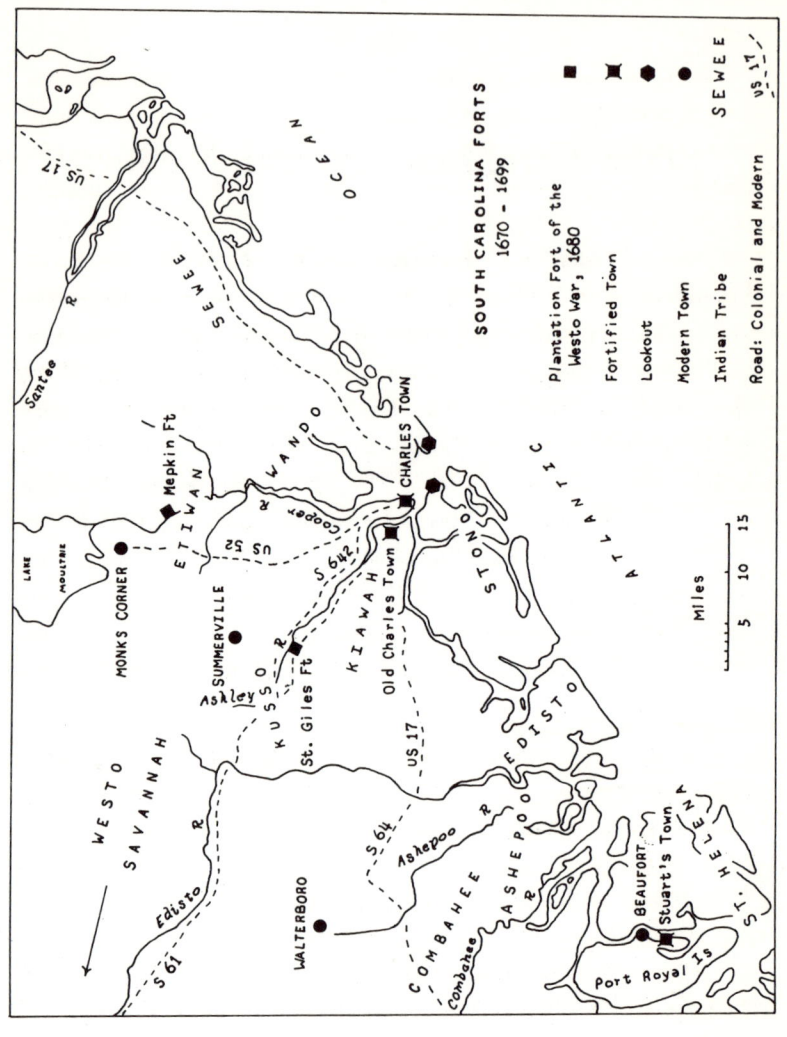

against warlike Indians was the use of even more warlike Indians.

Compounding the problem of dealing with the numerous Indian tribes was the presence of the Spaniards who had been established in Florida since 1565. The Spaniards claimed all the land south of Charles Town and demonstrated their desire to retain that area by destroying the two-year old Scottish settlement of Stuart's Town on Port Royal Island in 1686. The Spaniards had once maintained a chain of garrisoned missions along the Atlantic coast extending as far north as the Santee River. The missions maintained a large number of Christianized Indians under Spain's influence. The fatal military weakness of these Indians was their lack of firearms which the Spaniards refused to sell them. Between 1680 and 1684 Indians from the interior, newly armed with muskets and encouraged by their South Carolina traders, methodically destroyed the remaining missions located on the coast of present Georgia.

In a little over a decade the Indian trade had been developed to such an extent that several tribes condescended to do South Carolina's bidding strictly for the privilege of buying guns, blankets, and other goods in exchange for deerskins. The trade continued to expand to include the interior tribes, and by 1696 entire towns began moving closer to South Carolina in order to be nearer the source of the coveted trade goods. The government used these new found allies in her attacks against Spanish Florida. During the early part of Queen Anne's War (1701-1713) small numbers of South Carolinians led large Indian armies in the devastation of western Florida, and a large scale, but unsuccessful attack was conducted against the principal Spanish settlement at Saint Augustine.

Indian allies were used for defense as well as offense. By about 1703 friendly Indian towns formed two quarter circles along the frontier providing an active barrier against in-

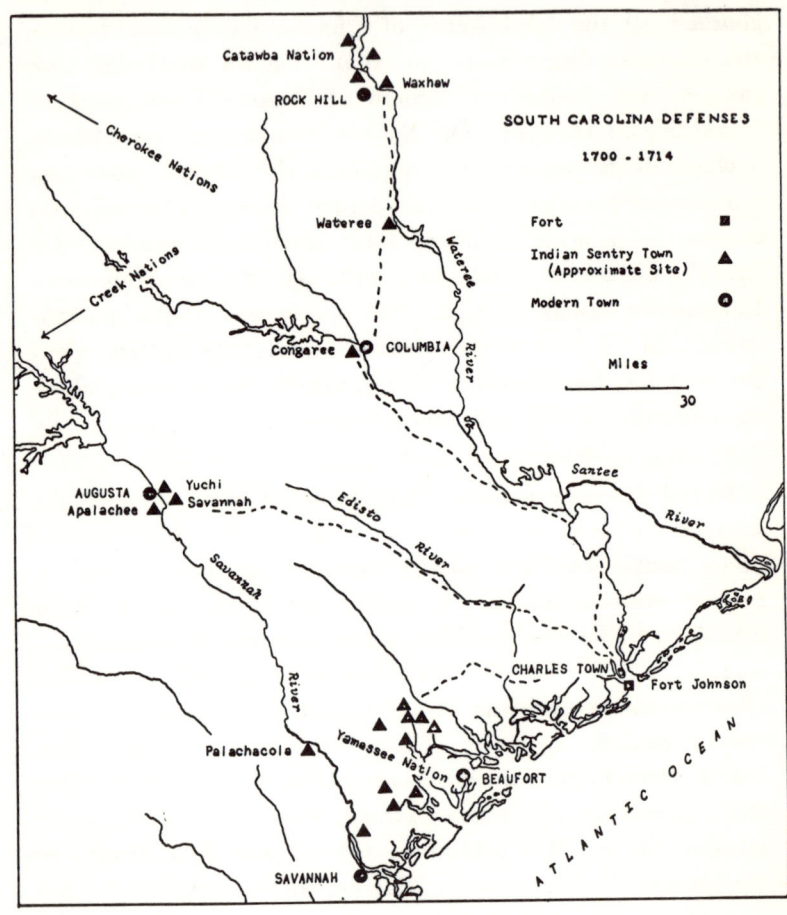

trusions by Spanish and French allied Indians. The outer quarter circle included some of the largest nations in the southeast. In and around the Smoky Mountains were the Cherokees. On the Oconee River in present Georgia were the Lower Creeks, and along the Coosa and Tallapoosa Rivers in present Alabama were the Upper Creeks. Far to the west near the Mississippi were the most loyal and best fighters, the Chickasaws. The inner circle was composed of a number of independent but very warlike towns. These "sentry-towns," villages of huts surrounded by palisades, protected the major entrance into the colony. To the north on the Wateree River were Waterees, Waxhaws, and the Catawba Nation. On the Congaree River were the Congarees. At the falls of the Savannah River were Savannahs, Yuchis, and Apalaches. On the lower Savannah were Palachacolas. Between the Combahee and the lower Savannah rivers were the ten towns of the Yamassee Nation.

As early as 1702 Spain and France began planning an invasion of South Carolina. In anticipation of the attack the South Carolinians built new fortifications around Charles Town, which had been moved from Albemarle Point to its present site, and placed handfuls of men as lookouts along the coast. The long awaited attack materialized in August 1706 when a combined Spanish and French fleet carrying Spanish soldiers attempted to capture Charles Town. The South Carolina militia and friendly Indians repulsed two landing parties in the harbor area taking two hundred and thirty prisoners, and a ragtag South Carolina flotilla drove off the enemy fleet. Alarms were raised throughout the remainder of the war, but additional attacks were not forthcoming. Charles Town was provided with the additional defense of Fort Johnson, built at the entrance of the harbor in 1708.

The excellent system of defense based on protection from Indian sentry-towns unfortunately began a slow deterioration. The South Carolina traders who lived in the towns operated beyond the law, ignoring all the government's attempts to reform them. Many cheated with false weights and measures, treated the warriors disdainfully, and extended credit until the individual balances reached an unpayable amount. South Carolina's practice of enslaving enemy Indians had fostered an attitude of distrust. Finally, in 1715, at the Lower Creeks' instigation, the warriors of the sentry-towns began the Yamassee War by murdering their traders, thereby cancelling their debts. They quickly followed this with large-scale attacks against the frontier which now extended east to the Santee River, north to the big bend in the Edisto River, and west to Combahee River and Port Royal Island.

The first blow was a surprise attack in April during which the Indian agent and several traders were killed in the Yamassee town of Pocotaligo near the present village of that name. Next, the Yamassees attacked the plantations on Port Royal and St. Helena islands, but most of the local settlers escaped to a ship moored in Port Royal harbor. Other Yamassees crossed the Combahee River and destroyed the plantations eastward to Edisto River, killing and capturing about one hundred people. All over the colony settlers gathered their essential household goods and fled to plantations of local militia commanders and prominent landowners, or to the houses of their ministers. A crude palisade of logs was quickly planted around the houses and nearby outbuildings to form temporary forts. The most prominent of the private plantation forts were Reverend Thomas Hasell's fort on the East Branch of Cooper River, Thomas Broughton's at Mulberry on the West Branch, Reverend Claude de Richbourg's in the French Huguenot settlements on the Santee River, George Chicken's on Back River, and John Jackson's on the Edisto River.

The Yamassees were quickly dealt with. A militia force marched into the Yamassee country, laying waste their towns and defeating their war parties. The warriors were soon forced to withdraw their families west of the Savannah River from where they continued to conduct raids.

In May the government raised a standing provincial army and ordered it to garrison six widely spaced forts around Charles Town. They were located on William Ford's plantation near Wando River to the east; Benjamin Schenckingh's cowpen (ranch) on Santee River to the north-northwest; Wassamassaw, Ralph Izard's cowpen, to the northwest; Richard Godfrey's plantation on Ashley River also to the northwest, but at a closer distance; and near James LaRoche's Bridge on Johns Island to the southwest. By now the other sentry-towns had joined the war against the colony, and in late May the warriors of the northern towns ambushed a large mounted force near the Santee, killing and capturing about thirty men. Shortly afterward these same Indians attacked and destroyed Schenckingh's fort. The northern Indians' major depredations were brought to an end in June when Captain George

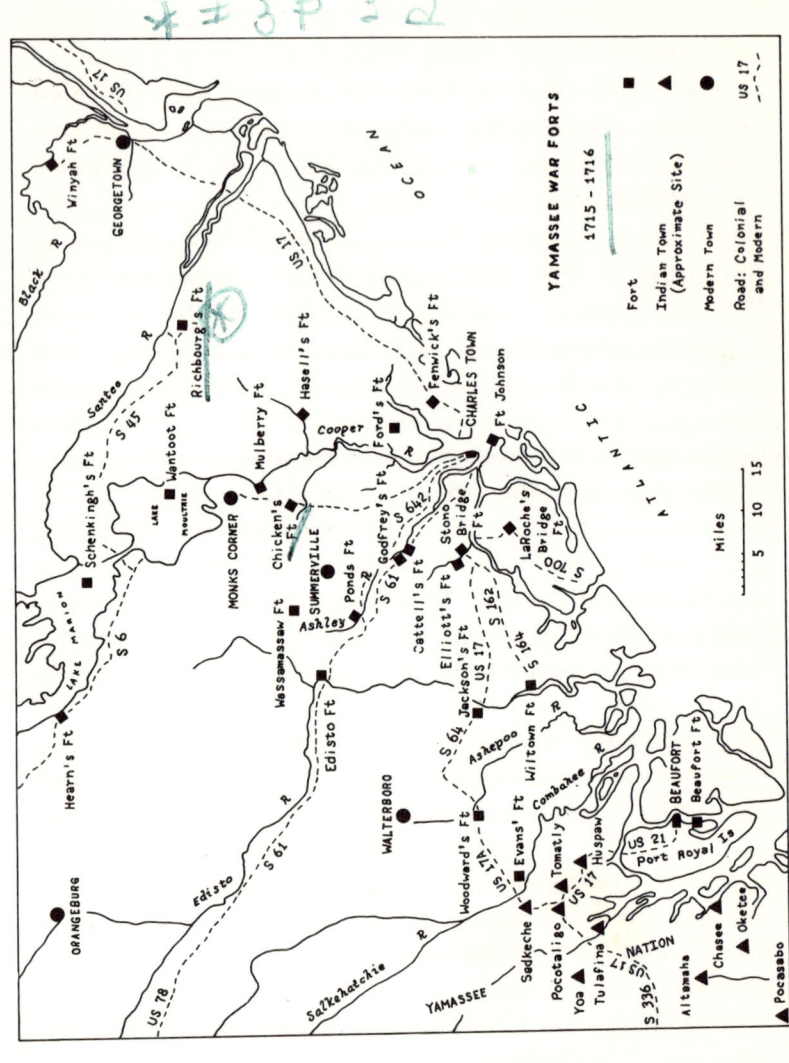

Chicken's militia company defeated them in open battle not far north of the Goose Creek settlements.

In July Indians from the upper Savannah River crossed the Edisto and razed the countryside eastward to the Ashley before withdrawing. The frontier was now tightly drawn around Charles Town.

It was apparent that the army garrisons were too widely spaced to provide mutual support to one another or to prevent war parties from penetrating the frontier. In August a complete reorganization of frontier defense was instituted. The army, which now included South Carolinians and their slaves, friendly Indians, Virginians, and North Carolinians, was to total fourteen hundred men divided into three regiments to guard the north, west, and south portions of the frontier. The regiments were garrisoned in a number of forts which formed a screen around the settlements between the Edisto and Santee rivers, protecting the settlers while they harvested their crops. The army was stationed as follows: sixty men in Robert Fenwick's plantation fort near Wando River; four hundred men north of Charles Town with headquarters at Wantoot Fort, Pierre de St. Julian's plantation fort on the upper Cooper River; one hundred men with riverboats at Edisto Fort on James Rawlings' plantation at the big bend of Edisto River; forty scouts with their scout boats at Wiltown village fort on the lower Edisto; two hundred men at the Ponds Fort on Andrew Percival's plantation located on the upper Ashley River; one hundred men in Peter Cattell's plantation fort on the middle Ashley; two hundred men in Thomas Elliott's fort on Rantowles Creek; two hundred men in a fort guarding

Stono Bridge on John Beamer's Stono River plantation; and one hundred men in a fort guarding James LaRoche's bridge connecting Wadmalaw and Johns islands. The scale of Indian attacks was soon reduced to small raids and ambushes.

The hostile tribes had deserted their sentry-towns on the frontier. The Congarees, Waterees, and Waxhaws had fled temporarily to the Catawba Nation. The lower Creeks had withdrawn to their old haunts on the Chattahoochee River and the Apalachees, Savannahs, Palachacolas, and Yuchis had joined them. The Yamassees had withdrawn to Florida and joined the Spaniards.

By November, with the crops harvested, a large portion of the army assembled at Ponds Fort for an attack on the Creek Nations, the instigators of the war. The strategy was to march northwest to the now deserted Savannah Town near present Augusta, Georgia, and rendezvous with a large force of Cherokees who were professed allies. It was planned that the army would then move against the Lower Creeks while a few soldiers and the Cherokees marched on the Upper Creeks. Upon arriving at Savannah Town the army constructed Fort Moore to guard the principal western entrance into South Carolina. The Cherokees did not rendezvous at Savannah Town as planned, however, and the army immediately marched into the Cherokee Nations to compel their allegiance. By January 1716 the Cherokees decided to ally with the South Carolinians, but the planned expedition against the Creeks was not undertaken. In February most of the army marched back to the settlements and was dispersed among the garrisons around Charles Town.

In March 1716 the army garrisons were reduced to six. Guarding the western entrance into the colony was Fort Moore. Blocking the intracoastal waterways to the southwest was Beaufort Fort on Port Royal Island with the colony's scout boats. An inner ring of garrisons began at a fort on John Hearn's plantation on Santee River. Edisto Fort was retained. The invasion route between Palachacola and Charles Town was guarded by a fort on John Woodward's plantation at the head of Ashepoo River and another fort on Rowland Evans' plantation at the head of Combahee River.

The raids and ambushes continued. By fall the government began using a few militia rangers (frontier horsemen) to patrol along the critical northern entrance into the colony. Finally, in December, the defensive system was again reorganized. A stationary garrison was maintained at Fort Moore and scout boats continued to be stationed at Beaufort Fort. Charles Town's immediate protection was furnished by three divisions, or companies, of rangers totaling about fifty men who were supposed to maintain patrols between their bases. The Northern Rangers were probably stationed at Hearn's fort; the Western Rangers were at Edisto Fort; and the Southern Rangers were at Woodward's fort.

This system was modified in December 1717. An additional garrison was ordered for Congaree Town, but the fort wasn't built for almost a year. One of the two scout boat crews at Beaufort was ordered to build and garrison a new fortification, subsequently named Passage Fort, further south on Daufuskie Island. The Southern Rangers were moved from Woodward's fort to a place on the Savannah River opposite deserted Palachacola Town where a crude palisade fort was apparently constructed. In 1718, with relative calm on the frontier, the rangers were discharged, but the other garrisons and the scouts were retained.

Until 1721 Fort Moore, Fort Congaree, and perhaps a small fort at Palachacola served as the government's factories, or Indian trading centers. Congaree Fort was abandoned in 1722 after the government withdrew from the Indian trade.

Meanwhile, the French in Louisiana had taken full advantage of the Yamassee War to establish an influence with South Carolina's old allies. In 1717 the Alabama faction of the Upper Creeks allowed the French to build and garrison Fort Toulouse among their towns. The French were determined to connect their provinces of Canada and Louisiana with a string of garrisoned forts thereby encircling the English colonies. No less obvious was Spain's intention to destroy South Carolina at the first opportunity. In 1720 John Barnwell, South Carolina's most experienced soldier, appeared before the British Board of Trade in London and argued for countermoves against Spain and especially against French expansion. He recommended that the British counteract France's strategy by building and garrisoning a number of forts on the frontier to block French moves and protect those Indians allied to England. The most critical area in the southeast, he believed, was the Altamaha River in present Georgia. The French reportedly intended to occupy that waterway in order to gain access from the Atlantic Ocean into the Creek Nations and

South Carolina, 1670–1775

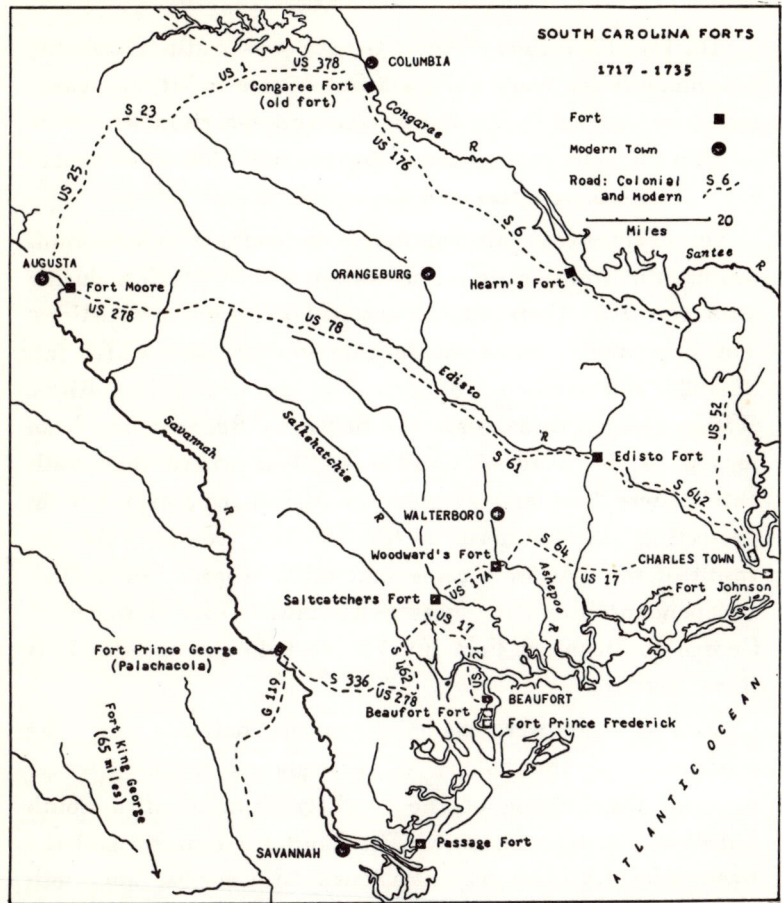

to cut those nations off from English trade. The Board agreed to fortify the mouth of that river and provide a garrison consisting of a regular Independent Company of Foot. In 1721 Barnwell and the colony's scouts built Fort King George near present Darien, Georgia, and the Independent Company was in garrison there by the following year.

During 1723 Fort Prince George was built across the Savannah River from old Palachacola Town. It was garrisoned by rangers called the Palachacola Garrison who were to prevent war parties from crossing the lower Savannah into the southern settlements.

The Yamassees had continued to conduct minor raids against the frontier since the war of 1715-1716, but during 1726 and 1727 their attacks reached alarming proportions. The Company of Southern Rangers was recruited in the fall of 1726 and stationed at Pon Pon on the Edisto River. Within two or three years the Southern Rangers had been moved to the head of Combahee River where they built Saltcatchers Fort and assisted the Palachacola Garrison in protecting the southern portion of the frontier. As the result of the Yamassee raids, and other reasons, the British Independent Company was withdrawn from Fort King George to Beaufort Fort in 1727 to help protect the Port Royal settlers.

Few changes were made in frontier defenses until the settlement of the colony of Georgia in 1733. Georgia assumed the defense of the southern frontier with South Carolina's initial assistance. The Southern Rangers and the scout boat *Carolina* were stationed in Georgia, and both units were later taken into Georgia pay. In 1735 Georgia assumed responsibility for the Palachacola Garrison at Fort Prince George, and the British Independent Company moved to Georgia the following year. During the War of Jenkins' Ear (1739-1748) South Carolina and Georgia cooperated briefly in an unsuccessful attack on Saint Augus-

South Carolina, 1670–1775   15

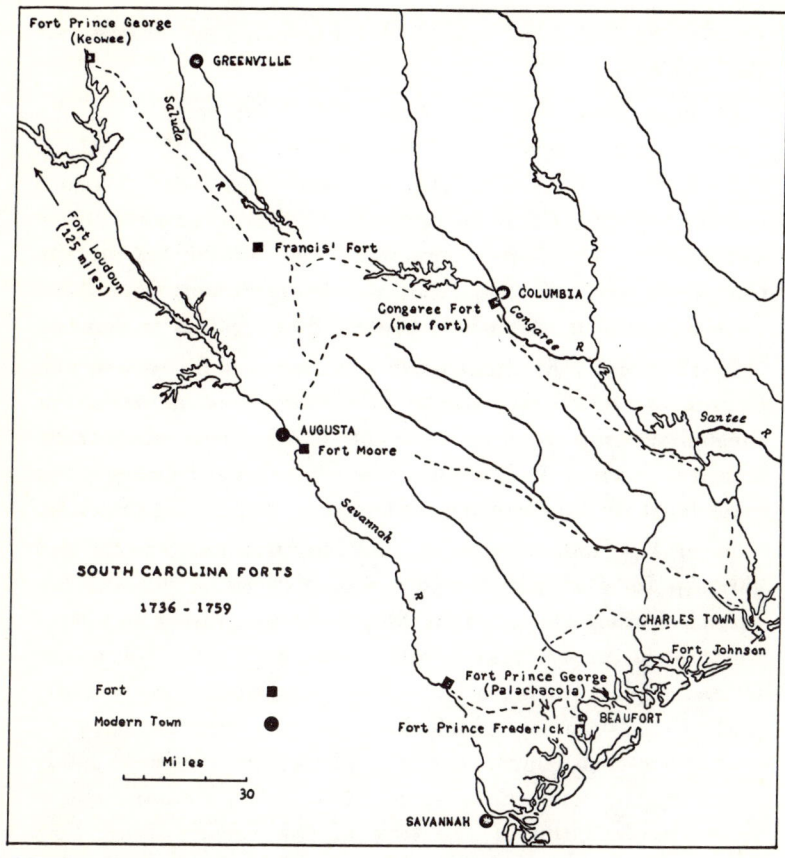

tine, but Georgia provided the principal defense against the Spaniards.

In 1746 South Carolina was fortunate to receive three British Independent Companies for frontier defense and protection against possible French attacks. One company was placed in garrison at Fort Prince Frederick which had replaced Beaufort Fort; another was stationed in Charles

Town; and the third was divided between Fort Moore and Fort Johnson.

Iroquois from the Ohio River had been enemies of the Catawbas who were now staunch friends of South Carolina. During the late 1740's the Iroquois began depredations against both the Catawba Indians and the northern frontier settlements. In 1748 a new fort was constructed at the Congarees and regulars from the Independent Companies were stationed there to help protect that exposed settlement.

In 1750 and 1751 small parties of Iroquois, Shawnees, and Cherokees conducted minor but numerous depredations throughout the colony, some of which took place near Charles Town and Beaufort. Many private frontier forts were built by the frontier settlers as a means of protection.

Several prominent officials had long wanted to build and garrison forts among the Cherokee Nations to prevent the French from gaining a foothold, to have a direct means of controlling the Cherokees, and to use as a place of refuge for the traders during a war. Governor James Glen ardently pushed the project which he believed was necessary to establish a firm control over the Cherokees who were lately becoming restless. Finally, in 1753, he personally supervised the building of the first of the fortifications, Fort Prince George, near the Lower Cherokee town of Keowee and garrisoned it with a detachment from one of the Independent Companies. Four years later, during the French and Indian War (1754-1763), Fort Loudoun was built across the Smoky Mountains among the Overhill Towns in present Tennessee. Its garrison included both British regulars and South Carolina provincials.

Relations with the Cherokee Nations had been deteriorating for some time. Like the period before the Yamassee War, the traders were cheating the warriors and were extending unlimited credit to them. The northern frontier settlements were now pushing into the Cherokee hunting lands, and French political activity in the towns inflamed the warriors. By the fall of 1759 the situation had grown so serious that Governor William Henry Lyttelton gathered a militia army and marched toward the Cherokee Nations as a show of force. A month after leaving Charles Town he arrived at Ninety Six, a small settlement on the edge of the frontier, and built a stockade fort to use as an army supply depot and as a refuge for the nearby settlers. The expedition reached Fort Prince George in early December where Lyttelton met with the Cherokee headmen. Part of the Cherokees desired war, but most wanted peace. By December soldiers of the expedition began deserting in such large numbers that Lyttelton was forced to sign hurriedly a peace treaty with the Cherokees and return to Charles Town. Twenty-two Indian hostages were kept in Fort Prince George to assure compliance with the treaty.

Cherokee restraint lasted only three weeks. During the latter part of January 1760 a force tried to enter Fort Prince George with concealed arms, but the commander foiled their plot. The Cherokees then began killing the British traders and laid seige to both Fort Prince George and Fort Loudoun. War parties devastated the frontier which now extended from near present Winnsboro westward to present Greenwood and McCormick. The majority of the settlements had a few days' or at least a few hours' warning. Most of the frontiersmen followed the practice of the Yamassee War and quickly constructed community forts where they took refuge. Some settlers made the mistake of loading their possessions on wagons and trying to outrun the war parties for the safety of the larger settlements. The Long Canes settlers, living in the vicinity of present McCormick, made a dash for Augusta, but a large war party caught them near Long Canes Creek and killed or captured about fifty people, mostly women and children. A similar disaster occurred further south on Stevens Creek. Those settlers who had taken refuge in stockade forts fared well even though some were briefly attacked. By April over twenty of these private forts were in existence. The most prominent were Thomas Barker's on Salkehatchie River, Thomas Fletchall's on Sandy River, Helm's on Wateree Creek, Lee's on Little River, Lyles' on Beaver Creek, Ninety Six, Edward Nixon's on Little River, John Pearson's on Broad River, Jacob Pennington's on Indian Creek, Jacob Brooks' on Bush River, John Tobler's on Savannah River, William Turner's on Saluda River, John Waggener's on Beaver Creek, and Fort William Henry Lyttelton on Enoree River.

After withdrawing to their towns to celebrate, the Cherokees again attacked the frontier in February beginning with another unsuccessful attempt on Fort Prince George. After the fort's commander was killed the garrison murdered the twenty-two hostages who were being held there and secretly buried them inside the fort. Following this, war parties burned several frontier farms and plantations along the Saluda River, but the population suffered little in their forts. The arrival of a force of rangers and militia prevented

South Carolina, 1670–1775

greater losses. Additional troops of rangers and companies of infantry were recruited and several companies of militia were placed in service. The private refugee forts began

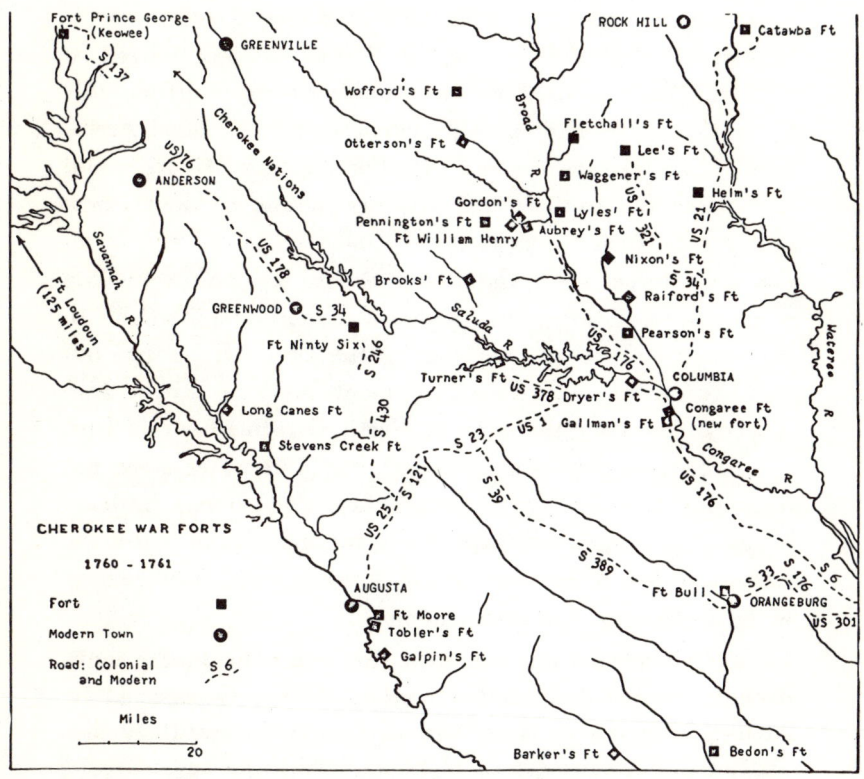

receiving government supplies of provisions and gunpowder to enable their civilian garrisons to remain on the frontier. Fort Loudoun, sitting three hundred and fifty miles across a high range of mountains from Charles Town, was doomed. It should have been evident before its construction that it could not be reinforced or supplied during an Indian war. The government decided to write Fort Loudoun off as a loss and concentrate on relieving Fort Prince George. In April twelve hundred regular British soldiers arrived in Charles Town to help defeat the Cherokees. In June this force of regulars and some provincials under Colonel Archibald Montgomery arrived at Fort Prince George and threatened the Indians with the destruction of their towns unless they sued for peace. The Indians ignored the warning, and three weeks later the expedition began moving northwest to destroy the towns of the Middle Settlement. No resistance was offered during the first fifty miles, but near Tassantee, a Middle Settlement town on Little Tennessee River near the present North Carolina-Georgia line, the Cherokees attacked. Although the Cherokees were not noted for their ability in battle they nevertheless inflicted losses on Montgomery's expedition, forcing him to withdraw. Leaving a few of his regulars in frontier forts, Montgomery withdrew to the northern colonies.

The Cherokees now pursued the war with a new confidence, turning their full attention to Fort Loudoun. By August 1760 the garrison had eaten the last of their provisions and was forced to surrender. The Cherokees agreed to allow the soldiers to march unharmed to Fort Prince George. However, on the second day of the garrison's withdrawal they were attacked. More than thirty were killed and the remainder were taken prisoner. The Cherokees now concentrated their energies on capturing Fort Prince George.

On the frontier several troops of rangers provided the outer screen of defense. One troop patrolled near the Congarees, two were responsible for the area between the Catawba and Broad rivers, two more between the Broad and Fort Ninety Six, and the final two between Fort Ninety Six and Fort Moore on the Savannah. The rangers were composed of undisciplined frontiersmen who sometimes caused much trouble by their poor behavior in the frontier forts. Regulars were stationed at Fort Ninety Six, now the base of operations, and the Congarees where an understrength provincial infantry regiment also resided. In January 1761 a new force of British regulars arrived in the colony under the command of Lieutenant Colonel James Grant. In May the force relieved the siege around Fort Prince George. When the Cherokees refused to appear to talk peace Grant marched northwest to raze their towns. He was attacked about two miles from the site of the previous year's battle. After three or four hours the Cherokees withdrew, allowing Grant's expedition to destroy fifteen towns and a large amount of food in the vicinity before withdrawing to Fort Prince George.

The major fighting was at an end, and negotiations began that summer. In December 1761 the Cherokees signed a treaty of peace which contained no great concessions. The Cherokees had been victorious throughout most of the war; however, after a year without trade goods they were practically destitute. They had become so dependent upon English guns, powder, knives, and woolens that they could scarcely exist without them.

After the end of the war, in 1762, Fort Lyttelton was completed to replace Fort Prince Frederick on Port Royal Island. Begun in 1758, it took almost five years to complete the new fort.

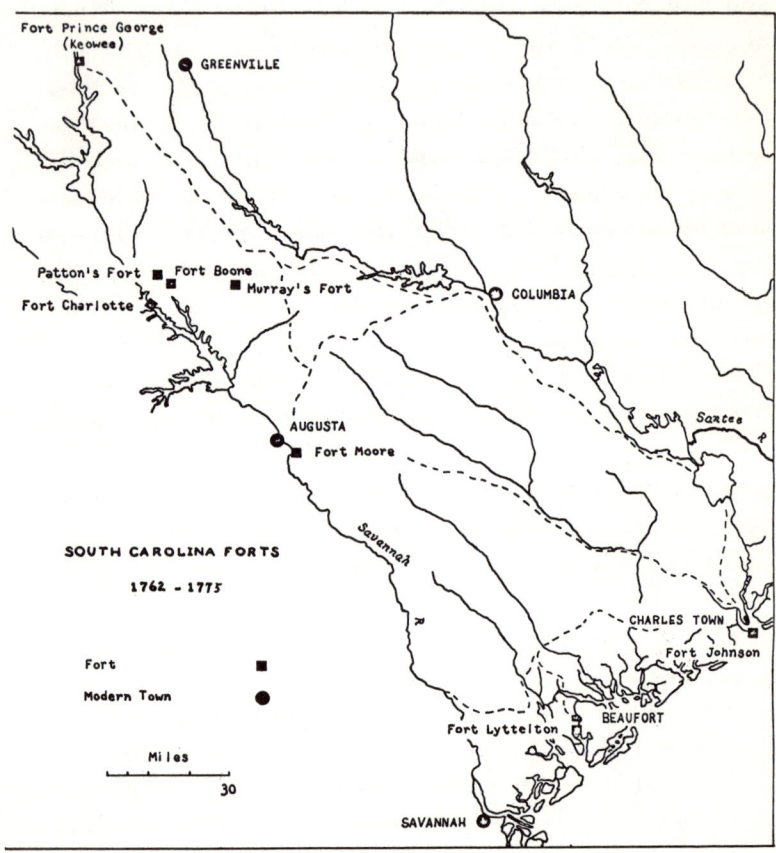

In early 1764 Creek Indian war parties began raiding the Long Canes settlements above Augusta. Several private frontier forts were constructed, and a provincial troop of rangers patrolled through the settlements. The frontier had long since passed beyond Fort Moore, so a new fortification, Fort Charlotte, was constructed in 1765 and 1766 further north near the Long Canes on the Savannah River. It was garrisoned with a detachment of British regulars from Fort Moore which was abandoned after fifty years of service.

A few regular soldiers continued to garrison the forts until 1768. A small provincial garrison continued at Fort Johnson, but with the disappearance of the threats of Spanish and French invasion the defenses of the province were generally allowed to fall into ruin.

A Description of the Forts and Their Garrisons

Two types of regular fortifications were used in South Carolina during the colonial period: European style earthwork forts and simple frontier forts with wooden walls.

Earthwork forts were normally constructed near the seacoast where it was likely that they would be subjected to bombardment by enemy ships or field artillery carried by an enemy landing force. However, several inland forts were also built in this style because of the possibility of their being subjected to bombardment by an invading French army from Louisiana.

The defensive works of an earthwork fort consisted of a dry moat, an earthen wall with a bastion or half-bastion at each corner, and a log palisade planted outside the moat, in the moat, or atop the earthen wall. Those works were designed to protect the garrison from cannon fire and to prevent an attacking force from gaining entrance into the fort. The bastions protruded beyond the walls allowing the defenders to fire in an arc of 270 degrees or more, raking the walls to either side. The forts' outlines were either rectangular or triangular.

Fort Johnson, built in 1708 and garrisoned throughout the remainder of the colonial period, serves as an excellent example. Protecting the entrance into Charles Town harbor,

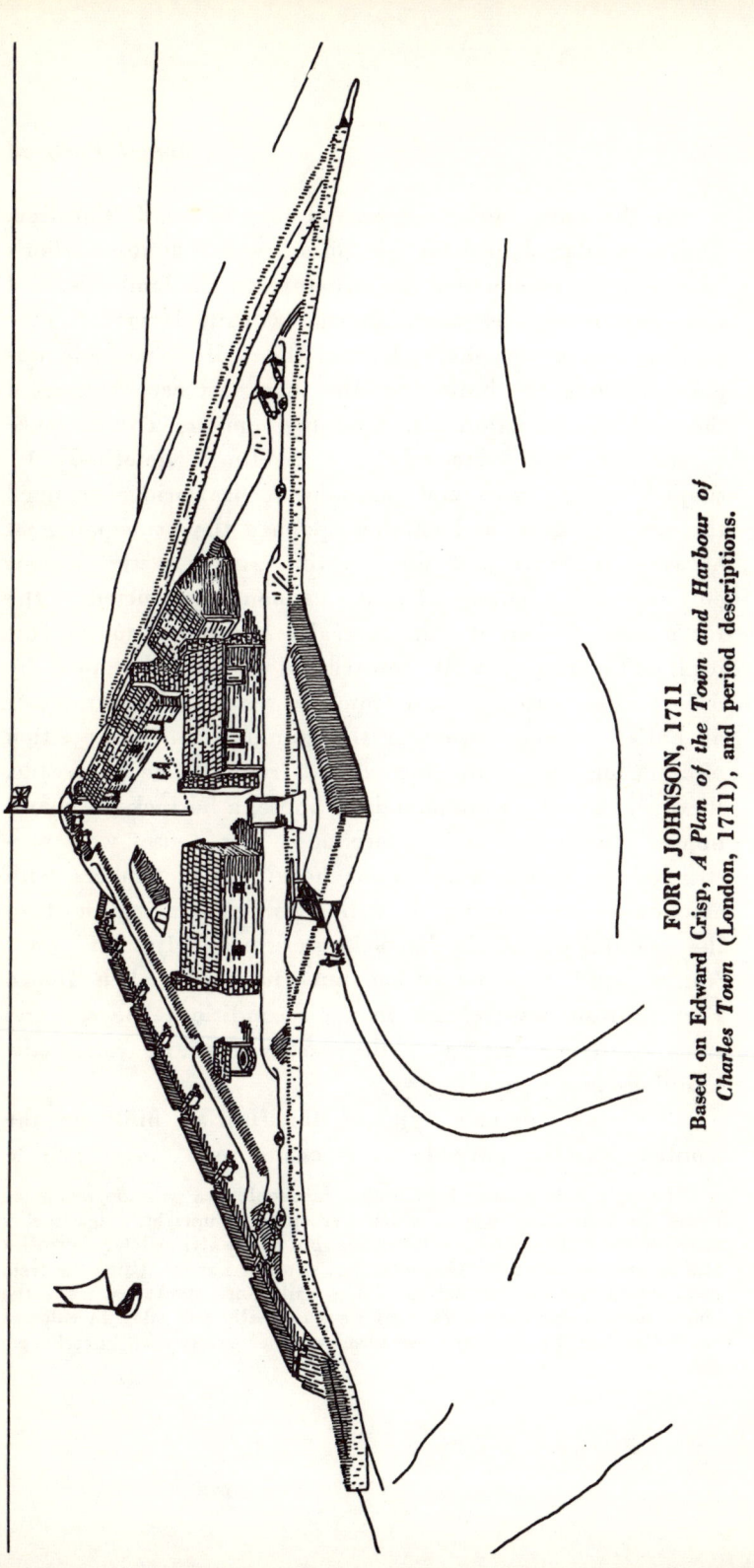

FORT JOHNSON, 1711
Based on Edward Crisp, *A Plan of the Town and Harbour of Charles Town* (London, 1711), and period descriptions.

it was the most important coastal fort in South Carolina. The triangular shaped fort sat on a low hill at the harbor's edge. A moat surrounded the structure on the land side, and the mud from the moat, alternated with layers of pine saplings and oyster shells, formed the wall. A palisade was planted along the bottom of the moat. At each corner of the wall was a bastion with mounted cannons. The entrance to the fort was protected by a ravelin, a detached "V" shaped earthen wall and palisade. A drawbridge spanned the ravelin's moat and another spanned the principal moat between the fort and the ravelin. Guarding the harbor entrance was a battery of heavy cannons constructed at the fort's base, or harbor side, several feet lower than the fort itself. The battery wall, constructed of earth retained by driven piles, was protected from the sea by a large number of ballast stones. Although the number and composition of buildings inside the fort varied from decade to decade, there was usually a commander's house, a barracks, a guardhouse, a magazine, and a storehouse. The houses were constructed by siding a frame of heavy, hewn timbers with clapboards and roofing it with shingles. During most of the colonial period the barracks were probably crude, post-framed, and clapboard-sided huts having earthen floors. Fort Johnson was seldom in good condition; the sea and rains constantly ate away the earthworks and rotted the buildings and palisade.

The most common type of fortification built on the frontier was the palisade or stockade fort.* Most private

* In eighteenth-century fortification terminology a palisade was a log fence, the individual logs of which were planted upright, a few inches apart. A stockade was also a log fence, but the individual logs were set against one another producing a tighter, stronger barrier. Using the technical definition, the frontier forts' log walls were stockades, while the fences surrounding earthwork forts were normally palisades. In colonial South Carolina, however, the two terms were generally used interchangeably.

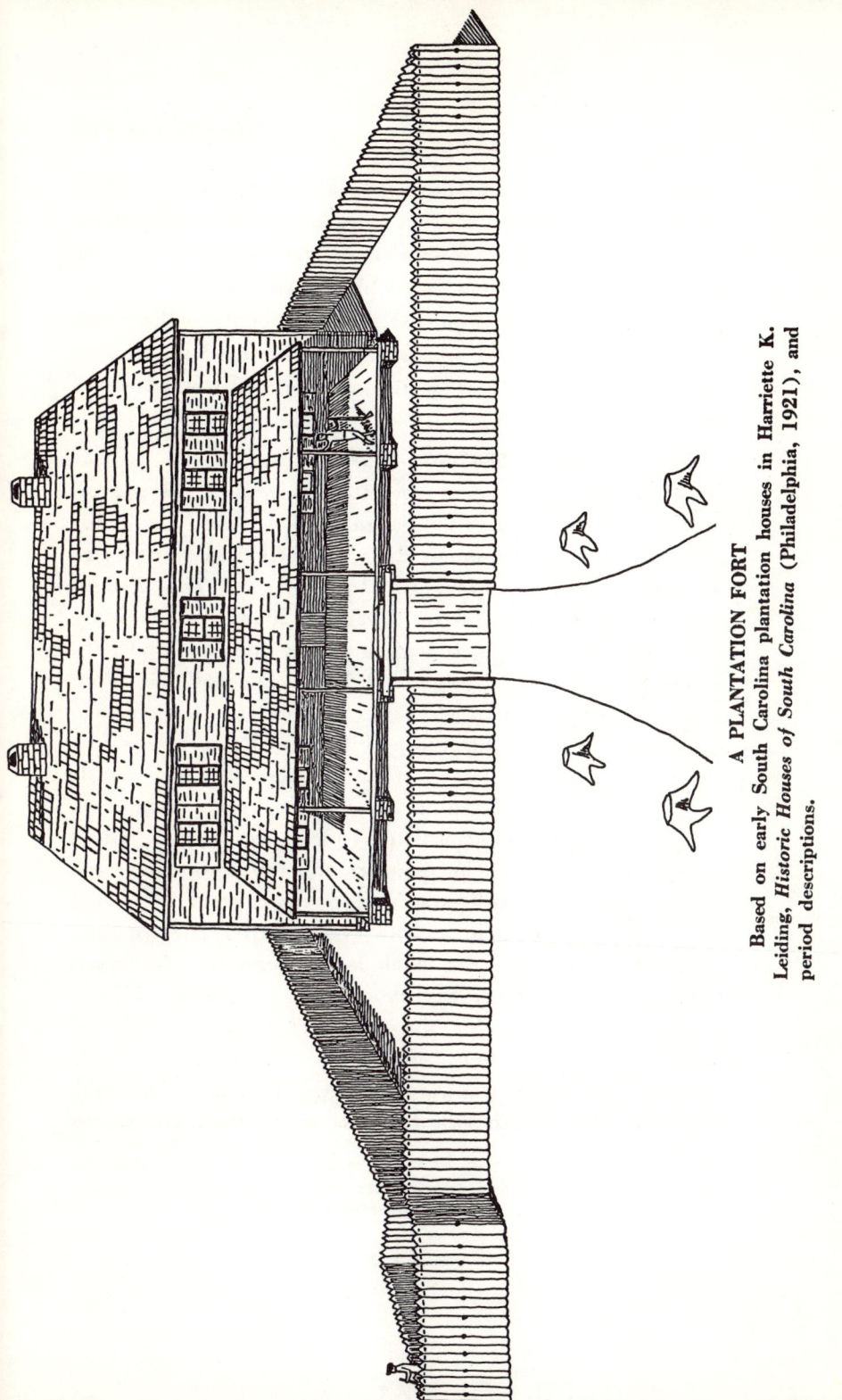

A PLANTATION FORT
Based on early South Carolina plantation houses in Harriette K. Leiding, *Historic Houses of South Carolina* (Philadelphia, 1921), and period descriptions.

plantation forts were of this type. They were usually built by hastily planting a stockade wall around a plantation house. Many regular frontier forts also used a stockade wall, while others used walls of plank. An earthen wall and a moat were seldom employed. Artillery could make short work of a wooden wall, but when used against Indians who had no artillery it was sufficient. Four inches of wood could stop most musket balls of that period.

Fort Moore (1715-1766), near Augusta, was a typical army frontier fort. Its purposes were to protect the nearby Indian trading center called Savannah Town, or New Windsor, and to guard Savannah Path, the principal route from the Creek Indian Nations to Charles Town. This flimsy, wooden fort overlooked the Savannah River from a bluff two hundred feet high. It was about one hundred and fifty feet square. The wall, only about four and a half feet high, was constructed by nailing planks horizontally to the inside of posts which were planted at intervals of five to ten feet around the fort's perimeter. (In 1747 the wall was rebuilt to a height of about ten to fifteen feet with a banquette, or platform walkway, constructed along the inside.) Light cannons were mounted on platforms in the bastions at each corner of the fort, and each bastion was covered by a shed roof to protect the sentries and cannons from the weather. Buildings inside the fort included a commander's house, barracks, storehouses, a guardhouse, a corn crib, a well, and a magazine. Except for the commander's house and the storehouses most of the buildings were probably huts. Although Fort Moore was very important to South Carolina's frontier defense, throughout much of its existence it was

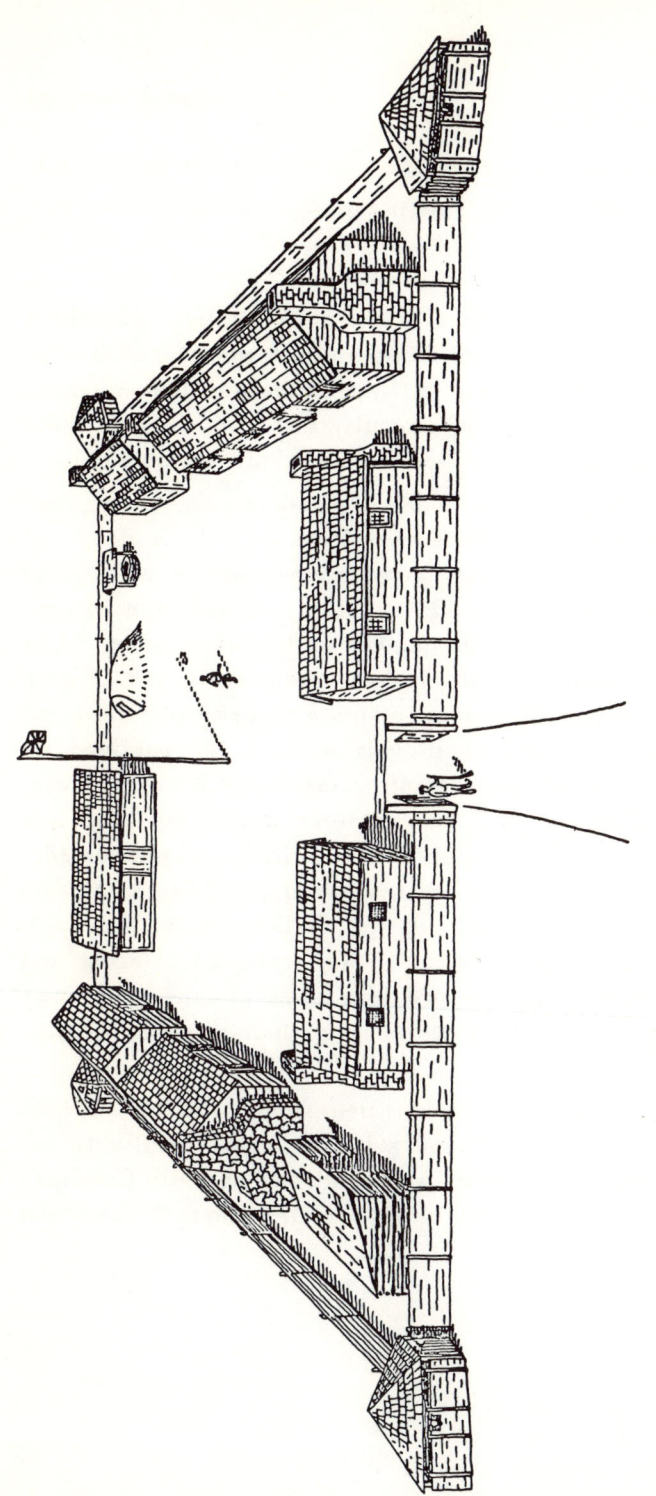

FORT MOORE, 1724
Based on period descriptions.

in poor repair and offered little protection for its garrison.

The forts' garrisons usually performed the construction and repair work for which they were paid extra wages, although professional carpenters, sawyers, and other artisans were sometimes hired. Regular fortifications sometimes took a long time to build. Because of the Cherokee War and the lack of funds Fort Lyttelton's construction lagged for five years. Normally, a regular fort could be completed in a short time, but few were actually built within a year.

When compared to modern standards the living conditions in South Carolina's early forts can only be described as miserable. The crude barracks were cold in winter and hot in summer, leaked during rains, and were fire hazards when dry. Earthen walls quickly washed away under rains, and green palisades and clapboards quickly rotted. Within about five years of its construction a fort required complete rebuilding. People and animals were closely confined together inside the walls, creating extremely unsanitary conditions. Flies plagued the garrisons during the day and mosquitos swarmed at night. The nearby woods undoubtedly served as the latrine. When neighboring settlers and traders crowded into the forts during Indian alarm, smallpox, measles, and other diseases soon appeared. During wet weather the grounds turned into a sea of mud, and many forts having earthen walls became shallow ponds because of poor drainage.

The frontier forts were often flimsy structures which provided poor defenses and primitive living conditions, but they served their purpose well. Only two of South Carolina's forts were captured by Indians, and neither of these was taken by an attack; entrançe was gained into Schenckingh's Fort by trickery, and Fort Loudoun's garrison was starved into submission.

Until the late 1740's the majority of the soldiers who comprised the regular forts' garrisons were members of South Carolina's own provincial army. The army included garrison soldiers, scout boat crews, and mounted rangers, most of whom were recruited or drafted from the militia.

Garrison soldiers primarily acted as artillerymen whose principal duties were to guard their forts and man the cannons during an attack. The garrison units usually included only a small number of men. They were not expected to conduct operations outside the forts. Officers commanded the garrisons and were assisted by sergeants. Each fort normally included a gunner who was in charge of the fort's cannons and was responsible for their employment.

Scouts manned the colony's scout boats, a service that began about 1707 as an outgrowth of the lookout system and continued with few interruptions until 1764. Two boats with crews were normally maintained on duty. They were supposed to use their fort only as a base of operations, for their principal duty was to ply the intracoastal waterways on the lookout for the approach of waterborne Indian and Spanish raiding parties and runaway slaves. Usually one scout boat crew was supposed to patrol while the other crew provided a garrison for the base fort. Scouts **were basically** marines; they could fight from the boat with the aid of swivel-guns (light cannons), or land and fight on foot. Scout boats were light, strong, shallow draft, and very fast. They were large canoes, averaging about six feet by forty feet, constructed from large cypress logs. First a log was hollowed out and shaped, then the resulting dugout was sawed down the center lengthwise and a plank was fixed between the halves. Each boat carried at least one mast, usually Bermuda rigged, but the main propellants were large oars, four to twelve in number, each of which was manned by a scout. Each crew was commanded by an officer.

Rangers were soldiers whose duty was to patrol on horseback along the fringe of the frontier looking for escaped slaves or the approach of hostile war parties. They also used their small stockade forts only as bases. Half of each company was to patrol while the other half secured the fort. Rangers fought like dragoons, soldiers who rode horses to battle then dismounted and fought on foot. South Carolina began using rangers in late 1716 and continued the practice intermittently until 1764. During Indian wars the ranger service was often unpopular and men had to be drafted to fill the units. Frontier novices dreaded the extreme danger of living on the frontier, and experienced frontiersmen were reluctant to leave their families unprotected while they were in service. A standing ranger force proved to be the best method of protecting exposed sections of the frontier.

The scouts and rangers were instructed to make regular patrols along assigned sections of the intracoastal waterways or the frontier trails. However, patrolling was very unpopular because of the heat and cold, privation, hard work, and the absence of frequent enemy contact which resulted in a lack of incentive. Evidence suggests that regular patrols were conducted only during periods immediately following Indian raids.

In 1721 a British Independent Company of Foot, a regular infantry unit, was sent from England to help man South Carolina's defenses. A detachment from the 42nd Regiment in Georgia was later garrisoned in South Carolina for a few years. Three British Independent Companies were sent to the colony in 1746 and served in frontier garrisons for three years. Upon their disbandment in 1749 three new companies were formed and served until 1764. Three companies of the Royal American Regiment replaced the Independent Companies and served on the frontier until 1768.

The British regulars practiced a certain amount of musket and bayonet drill and conducted training in platoon maneuvers, but for the South Carolina provincial soldiers training was practically unknown. A small amount of musket practice and cannon crew drill were probably conducted, but platoon and company maneuvers were unnecessary. Garrison soldiers were not expected to fight outside the forts' walls, and the scouts and rangers operated in small, swift-moving units, conducting warfare like the Indians.

The most frequent work detail in the forts was guard duty which may have occurred two or three times a week for each soldier. Although guard duty was disliked, the most hated work details were cooking, cutting firewood, and carrying water.

Except during Indian wars and periods of alarm the garrisons spent as much time performing personal occupations as military duties. Soldiers farmed patches of corn, for which they were subsidized by the government, and raised black cattle. Although trading with the Indians was unauthorized, some bartering undoubtedly took place. Most of the garrison commanders maintained nearby plantations or cowpens (ranches) and operated general stores within their forts.

Neither military duties nor personal occupations were pursued at a fast pace. A primary reason for the soldiers' laziness was the unhealthy condition of the frontier. Lack of a well balanced diet, intestinal parasites, an excessive intake of rum, and fevers sapped their strength and kept them thin. The hot months of summer were particularly dangerous; mosquitoes, flies, bad water, and tainted food caused deaths by malaria, dysentery, typhoid, and other diseases.

The principal foods in the garrisons were corn (the staple) and beef. This was supplemented with vegetables and hogs purchased from local Indian towns, and by hunting and fishing. Soldiers seldom drank water when beer was available. An acceptable homemade beer was produced by mixing and boiling water, sassafras, pine needles, molasses, and corn.

Recreation and entertainment were homemade. Horse and boat racing were popular, and bets were made on the results. Holidays were spent in playing games, dancing, and drinking. Most punch houses, or taverns, of any size boasted at least one billiard table. Infrequent visitors to the forts provided the most welcome diversion by bringing a new face and the latest news from the outside world.

South Carolina paid her soldiers an acceptable wage, but it was sometimes hard to recruit frontiersmen since the job of packhorseman for the Indian traders always paid more. Some commanders increased their own pay by padding their muster rolls, thereby collecting the pay of nonexistent soldiers. Other artifices included enlisting their infant sons, requiring their soldiers to work on their plantations, and continuing deserters and dead men on the rolls. A similar practice, but one with a humane purpose, was continuing disabled soldiers on the rolls as a form of pension. Rangers usually received more pay than other soldiers; they were, however, required to provide their own horses and provisions. With few exceptions garrison soldiers, scouts, and rangers were not issued uniforms, but wore their own civilian clothing. The British regulars stationed in the colony wore the standard red uniform.

If living conditions in the frontier forts were crude, the soldiers who comprised the garrisons were no less so. Most were illiterate, and few practiced their religion. Their speech and mannerisms were vulgar, their bodies went unwashed, and their humor was crude and cruel.

Like most South Carolina frontiersmen the soldiers' greatest vice was drunkenness from rum punch, a mixture of rum and water. The favorite off-duty spots for soldiers were the punch houses which abounded in Charles Town, the lesser settlements, and even on the edge of the frontier. It became necessary for the government to pass laws regulating the conduct of punch house owners who were in the habit of extending unlimited credit. When their debts reached an excessive sum, soldiers deserted the service and the colony rather than attempt payment.

Although some soldiers had families at the forts the

lack of women on the remote frontier sometimes posed problems. However, Indian towns were established near most of the outlying forts, and the soldiers lived with Indian girls, both temporarily and permanently. The Indian warriors usually accepted the arrangements, if their wives were not molested, and the mistresses and wives of the soldiers provided a friendly link to the nearby towns. Like all young soldiers living with local women, they quickly went native, learning to speak some of the language and practicing many of the local customs.

Crude as the early South Carolina soldiers may have been, it must not be assumed that they were incompetent. Some of the units, like Captain James McPherson's Company of Southern Rangers (1726-1738), were small, but highly skilled military forces which served as a vital deterrent to Indian raids. The soldiers were inured to the harsh living conditions on the frontier, and after a period of experience they often learned to better the Indians at their own brand of forest warfare.

A List of the Principal Forts

The following forts were built and garrisoned in South Carolina during the period 1670-1775. The location, description, and a short history of each is included. Many of the colonial trails which connected the forts and settlements are traced or closely paralleled by modern highways. By comparing the trails marked on this booklet's maps with highways on a road map it is possible to drive an automobile along or near many of the former trails while visiting the old fort sites.

ASHEPOO FORT A private fort during the Cherokee War of 1760-1761 located near the head of Ashepoo River (Colleton County). The identification of the garrison and the exact location are unknown. The fact that a fort was built that far from the scene of action is an indication of the panic which resulted from the war. The principal danger in that area was the possibility of a slave uprising resulting from Cherokee successes.

AUBREY'S FORT A private frontier fort built on Samuel Aubrey's land located on the south side of Enoree River, ten miles southeast of present Whitmire (Newberry County). The fort was built in early 1760 at the beginning of the Cherokee War, but was soon abandoned when the refugee settlers apparently went to live in nearby Fort William Henry Lyttelton which was probably a larger and stronger fortification.

BARKER'S FORT A private frontier fort during the Cherokee War of 1760-1761 on Thomas Barker's land located on the west side of the head of Salkehatchie River. The exact location is unknown, but it was probably east-northeast of present Allendale (Allendale County).

BEAUFORT FORT (PORT ROYAL FORT) It was possible for Indian and Spanish raiders to travel from Florida to Charles Town by canoe via the Inland Passage, present Intracoastal Waterway, without sailing upon the open sea. Beginning in 1707 scout boats were stationed on Port Royal Island to keep a lookout for hostile movement into the settlements by way of the Inland Passage. In April 1715 the Yamassee Indians, whose towns were north and west of Port Royal Island, conducted a series of attacks, driving the South Carolina settlers from the southwestern portions of the colony. Despite the exodus of settlers and the withdrawal of the scout boats to Willtown, a small garrison of militia built a fortification on Port Royal Island and remained there throughout 1715 to observe movements of war parties by water. In March 1716 two scout boats were ordered restationed there to prevent war parties from entering the colony by canoe. Beaufort Fort, also called Port Royal Fort, was probably located south of Beaufort either on Spanish Point or on the site of the present U. S. Navy Hospital one and a half miles farther south (Beaufort County). The fort continued to serve as a scout boat base. During 1721 and part of 1722 the Independent Company of Foot, a regular British infantry unit, was stationed there. In 1724 the fort was rebuilt. It probably consisted of earthen walls surrounded by a palisade. In 1727 the Independent Company was again placed there after being withdrawn from Fort King George near present Darien, Georgia. In 1734 a new fortification, Fort Prince Frederick, was completed to replace dilapidated Beaufort Fort.

BEDON'S FORT   A Cherokee War private frontier fort apparently located between Little Salkehatchie River and Buckhead Creek near present Smoaks (Bamberg or Colleton County).

FORT BOONE   A private frontier fort built on Patrick Calhoun's plantation called Cane Hill located about eight miles southeast of present Calhoun Falls (McCormick County). It was constructed in early 1764 to protect the settlers near Calhoun Creek from raids which had lately been instigated by Creek Indians against the Long Canes settlements. It contained one hundred and forty refugee settlers. For six months during 1764 Captain Calhoun commanded a troop of rangers which were stationed there.

BROOKS' (RHALL'S) FORT   A private frontier fort built during the Cherokee War of 1760-1761 on Jacob Brooks' land located on the west side of Bush River near present Newberry (Newberry County). The fort was attacked by a Cherokee war party in March 1760. A man caught outside was killed, but the garrison left their fort and engaged the Indians in open battle, driving them off.

CATTELL'S FORT   A fortified house on Peter Cattell's

Ashley Hill plantation located on the west bank of Ashley River, thirteen and one-half miles northwest of Charles Town (Charleston County). It contained an army garrison from August 1715 to March 1716.

CHARLES TOWN'S FORTIFICATIONS During 1670 and 1671 the first South Carolina colonists protected their settlement at Albemarle Point with a moat and a palisade fence. When Charles Town was moved to its present site in 1680 it was likewise fortified. The fortifications were soon expanded and improved until the town was surrounded by earthworks and palisades encompassing an area about a mile north and south, and a half mile east and west along Cooper River in the southeastern part of present Charleston. The Charles Town militia provided the fortifications' garrisons in time of emergency, but a full-time Captain of the Fort, or Commander of the Fortifications, was appointed by the government to care for the cannons, gunpowder, etc. The principal components of the fortification were six bastions, diamond or triangular shaped works, and two half moons, works in the shape of a half circle. The bastions and half moons, constructed of earth, wood, and bricks, protruded beyond the walls. Each was actually a separate fort containing its own cannons and assigned militia garrison. Blake's and Granville's Bastions were located on the southeast side of the fortification near the intersection of present Water and East Bay streets. Ashley's Bastion stood near the intersection of present Church and Water streets. Colleton's Bastion was located near the intersection of Meeting and Tradd streets. Johnson's Covered Half Moon (actually a demilune covering the gate) was near the intersection of

Meeting and Broad streets. Carteret's Bastion was located near the intersection of Meeting and Cumberland streets.

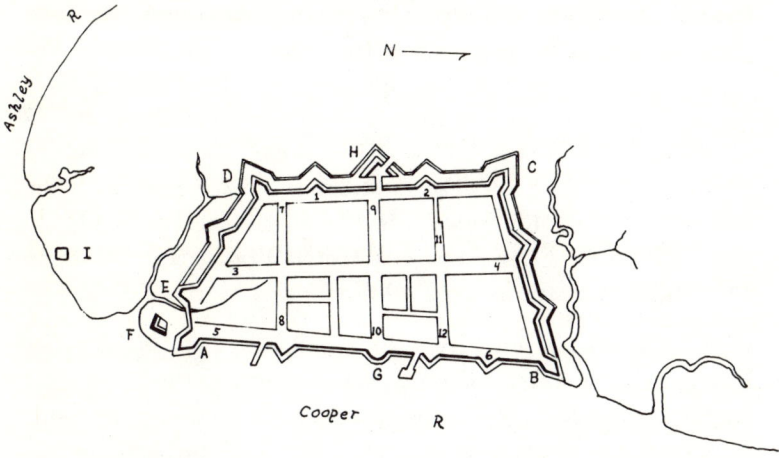

CHARLES TOWN'S FORTIFICATIONS, 1695-1745

A: Granville's Bastion
B: Craven's Bastion
C: Carteret's Bastion
D: Colleton's Bastion
E: Ashley's Bastion
F: Blake's Bastion
G: Half Moon
H: Johnson's Covered Half Moon (a Demilune)
I: Watch House (later Broughton's Battery)

1- 2: Meeting House Street
3- 4: Church Street
5- 6: Bay Street
7- 8: Tradd Street
9-10: Broad Street
11-12: Queen Street

A modified tracing of Edward Crisp's Plan of Charles Town, 1704

Craven's Bastion was near the east end of Market Street. And a half moon was located on the waterfront near the east end of Broad Street. In addition to the bastions and half moons, a watch house, later replaced by Broughton's Battery, and entrenchments were located at White Point Gardens on the southern point of the peninsula. Except for minor extensions and constant repair work this remained the composition of Charles Town's fortifications until 1745 and 1746, when a new wall with five bastions was constructed from Craven's Bastion, at the east end of Market Street, south-southwest almost to Ashley River near the west end of present Beaufain Street. In September 1752 a hurricane destroyed most of the town's fortifications, necessitating extensive repairs. After Britain defeated France and Spain in 1763 the fortifications were allowed to go to ruin.

FORT CHARLOTTE By 1764 the South Carolina frontier had long since extended northwest beyond Fort Moore near Augusta. Accordingly, a new fort was planned for the Long Canes area to protect that most exposed of the settlements. By December 1766 the new fortification, Fort Charlotte, was completed on the west bank of Savannah River a half mile below its junction with Broad River (McCormick County). It was a small but strong fort built in the form of a rectangle fifty by forty feet. Field stones cemented together formed a wall two feet thick and probably about five feet high. Two bastions were constructed on the northwest end. It sat on a fill of sand in the midst of a swamp about fifty yards from the Savannah. Fort Moore's British garrison, a platoon from the Royal American Regiment, was transferred to Fort Charlotte. The British garrison was withdrawn about 1768, and the fort was abandoned until the revolution. Today the site is covered by Clark Hill Reservoir.

CHICKEN'S FORT A fortified house on George Chicken's plantation located nine miles northeast of present Summerville (Berkeley County). Captain Chicken's company of Goose Creek militia used the fort as a base throughout the Yamassee War of 1715-1716. On June 13, 1715, Chicken's company met and defeated a large war party which had destroyed Schenckingh's Fort a few days before. The company was part of the army which marched to the Cherokee Nations in November 1715.

CONGAREE FORT (old fort)   Congaree Town was a small village of Indians of the Catawba tribe who lived on the west side of Congaree River near present Columbia. Congaree Town served as a sentry-town protecting the northern entrance into South Carolina until the Yamassee War of 1715-1716 when these Indians assisted the other frontier tribes in their attacks against the settlements. Following the war they fled to live with the Catawbas. In 1718 Captain Charles Russell and an army unit built and garrisoned Congaree Fort located in present Cayce on the east bank of Congaree Creek one and a half miles above its mouth (Lexington County). It was apparently an earthen walled structure, except that the west side, which butted against Congaree Creek, was protected only by a palisade. The opposite side had a bastion at each corner, and a ravelin protected the gate on the north side. A moat with a palisade planted in the bottom may have surrounded the fort on the land side. The fort served as a trading factory, a government Indian trading post, until 1721. The garrison's strength varied between thirteen and twenty-one men. In 1722 the fort was abandoned.

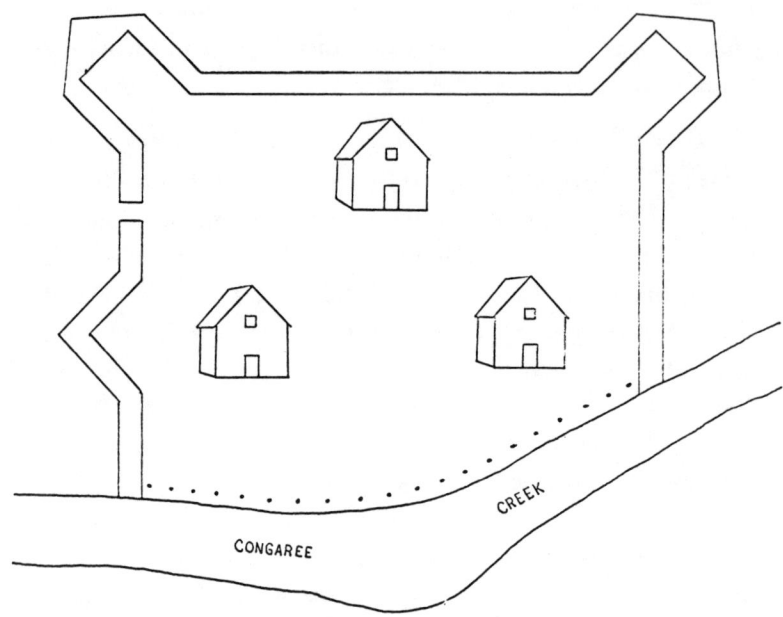

CONGAREE FORT (old fort), 1718-1722
A rough plan from "Sketch Map of the Rivers Santee, Congaree, Wateree, Saludee, etc., with the Road to the Cuttauboes."
Courtesy of the British Public Record Office.

CONGAREE FORT (new fort) Iroquois warriors living near the Ohio River began committing murders and other outrages along the Congaree section of the frontier in the late 1740's. A fort was constructed in 1748 to protect that area. It was apparently located on the west side of Congaree

River in present Cayce about two and one-half miles north-northwest of the old fort (Lexington County). It had earthen walls, a moat, and a palisade. British regular soldiers from one of the Independent Companies assigned to South Carolina were garrisoned there. In 1754 the fort's commander, Lieutenant Peter Mercier, led the garrison to Virginia where they joined George Washington's expedition to build a fort on the Ohio River. Mercier was killed by the French in the resulting Battle of Great Meadows.

DRYER'S FORT   A private frontier fort built on Godfrey Dryer's (Dreher) land during the Cherokee War. It was located on the south side of Saluda River about five and a half miles west of present Columbia (Lexington County). In May 1760 the fort contained one hundred and twenty-one women and children refugees.

EDISTO FORT   A fort built during the Yamassee War on James Rawlings' plantation called Edisto Bluff located on the east bank of the Edisto River near present Givhan's Ferry State Park (Dorchester County). The fort guarded Savannah Path, the strategic western entrance into the South Carolina settlements. An army unit was garrisoned there with river boats from May 1715 to December 1716. During the period December 1716 to June 1718 the Western Rangers (Westward Division of Rangers), a half dozen horsemen, were stationed there under Captain John Jones, an Indian trader. The rangers maintained communications between Charles Town and Fort Moore near present Augusta, Georgia. Captain Jones and some of his men rode three hundred miles to the Lower Creek Nation near present Columbus, Georgia, in the spring of 1717 to conduct peace negotiations.

ELLIOTT'S FORT A fortified house during the Yamassee War on the plantation owned by Thomas Elliott located on the west bank of Rantowles Creek twelve miles west of Charles Town (Charleston County). It was a local militia fort from April to August 1715, but from August 1715 to March 1716 it contained an army garrison.

EVANS' FORT A Yamassee War fort on Rowland Evans' plantation situated on the east side of Combahee River. The exact location is unknown, but it was probably east of present Yamassee (Colleton County). An army garrison was stationed there from March to December 1716.

FENWICK'S FORT A fortified house during the Yamassee War on Robert Fenwick's plantation located about eight miles northeast of Charles Town, just south-southwest of Boone Hall Plantation (Charleston County). Local militiamen probably garrisoned the fort during the period May to August 1715. From August 1715 to March 1716 it contained an army garrison.

FLETCHALL'S FORT A private frontier fort during the Cherokee War of 1760-1761 on Thomas Fletchall's (Fletcher) land located somewhere along the southeast side of Sandy River near present Chester (Chester County).

FORD'S FORT A fortified house on William Ford's plantation located on the west side of Wando River. The exact site is unknown, but it was probably about ten miles northeast of Charles Town (Berkeley County). This Yamassee War fortification contained an army garrison from May to August 1715, and probably contained local militia soldiers from August 1715 to the spring of 1716.

FRANCIS' FORT   A private frontier fort built by James Francis and other Ninety Six settlers in the spring of 1751 when small Iroquois war parties committed depredations along the frontier. The site was about three miles east of Greenwood (Greenwood County).

GALLMAN'S FORT   A private fort built on Henry Gallman's land during the Cherokee War of 1760-1761. Its location was on the north bank of Congaree Creek south of present Columbia (Lexington County).

GALPHIN'S FORT   A private frontier fort on George Galphin's plantation at Silver Bluff on the east bank of Savannah River, west of present Jackson (Aiken County). It was maintained during most of the Cherokee War of 1760-1761.

GODFREY'S FORT   A fortified house on the plantation owned by Richard Godfrey, presently known as Middleton Gardens, on the west bank of Ashley River, fourteen miles northwest of Charles Town (Dorchester County). It served as an army garrison from May to August 1715 during the Yamassee War.

GORDON'S FORT   A private frontier fort built during the Cherokee War of 1760-1761. It was located on the east side of Enoree River, about seven miles southeast of present Whitmire (Newberry County).

HASELL'S FORT   A private fort on Thomas Hasell's plantation called Pompion Hill located on the east bank of the East Branch of Cooper River, twelve miles southeast of present Moncks Corner (Berkeley County). Reverend Thomas Hasell was the Rector of St. Thomas Parish and many of his parishioners lived as refugees in his fort during much of the Yamassee War of 1715-1716.

HEARN'S FORT A Yamassee War fortification on John Hearn's plantation located on the west bank of Santee River about due west of present Orangeburg (Orangeburg County). In May 1715 a large war party of Catawba Indians and their allies raided the plantation and killed John Hearn. Shortly afterward the same war party ambushed a company of horsemen who were enroute to Hearn's plantation where they intended to build a fort. One third of the horsemen were killed and the remainder were routed. It was probably this same war party which destroyed Schenckingh's Fort. A fort was built and an army garrison was established at Hearn's plantation in March 1716 to guard the strategic northern entrance into the South Carolina settlements. The Northern Rangers (Northward Division of Rangers), a score of horsemen, were probably stationed there from December 1716 to June 1718.

HELM'S FORT A private frontier fort on the north side of Wateree Creek during the Cherokee War of 1760-1761. The exact location is unknown, but it was southwest of present Great Falls (Fairfield County).

INDIAN SENTRY-TOWNS A number of small, friendly Indian tribes established their towns near the principal entrances into South Carolina during the early 1700's and served as a defensive barrier against the inroads of Spaniards, French, and hostile Indians. Most of the sentry-towns were villages of wattle huts surrounded by a palisade wall. The material benefits derived from the Indian trade had in-

South Carolina, 1670–1775

duced the tribes to protect the frontier. The corrupt, immoral practices of the South Carolina traders, however, caused all the tribes to declare war in 1715. During the resulting Yamassee War the once friendly Indians devastated the frontier, deserted their sentry-towns, and fled to the interior. The following were the principal sentry-towns:

APALACHEE TOWN A Muskhogean division of Indians consisting of about one hundred and fifty warriors located on the east bank of Savannah River, southeast of present Augusta, Georgia (Richmond County, Georgia). These Indians formerly lived in western Florida under Spanish influence. In 1704 an army of South Carolinians and Creek Indians destroyed the Apalachee towns with their Spanish missions and removed three hundred Indians to the Savannah River to serve as a sentry-town.

CATAWBA NATION A tribe of Siouan stock consisting of about one hundred and twenty men living in several very small villages near present Catawba Lake (York and Lancaster Counties). This nation made peace with South Carolina following the Yamassee War, and its villages continued to serve as sentry-towns throughout the remainder of the colonial period. Although small, the Catawba Nation was very warlike and was involved in continual strife with the Iroquois living in New York and along the Ohio River.

CONGAREE TOWN A Catawba division of Indians consisting of about thirty men located near present Columbia on the west bank of Congaree River (Lexington County). Following the Yamassee War the Congarees joined the Catawba

Nation. Congaree Fort was built near the deserted town in 1718.

PALACHACOLA TOWN   Also called Apalachicola. They were a Hitchiti group of the Muskhogean division consisting of about one hundred warriors. The town was located on the west bank of Savannah River, about thirty-five miles north-northwest of present Savannah, Georgia (Effingham County, Georgia). Fort Prince George was constructed across the river from the deserted town in 1723. A decade after the Yamassee War a small band of Yuchi (Uchee) Indians established a sentry-town near the old town site and remained there until the 1740's.

SAVANNAH TOWN   A village of Shawnee Indians of the Algonquan stock. The town consisted of about sixty men located on the east bank of Savannah River approximately four miles southeast of present Augusta, Georgia (Aiken County). Fort Moore was built near the deserted town in 1716.

WATEREE TOWN   A Catawba division of Indians consisting of about forty men located northeast of present Winnsboro on the west bank of Wateree River (Fairfield County).

WAXHAW TOWN   A Catawba division of Indians consisting of about one hundred warriors located on the east side of Catawba River near present Fort Mill (York County).

YAMASSEE NATION   A Hitchiti group of the Muskhogean division consisting of about three hundred and fifty warriors divided among ten towns. These Indians had originally lived in Guale, present coastal Georgia, under Spanish influence. However, they revolted against the Spaniards beginning about 1684, and by 1703 they had all moved to the South Carolina frontier. Between ten and twenty miles northwest of present Beaufort were the towns of Pocotaligo, Huspaw, Yoa, Sadkeche, and Tomatly. Ten to thirty miles southwest of Beaufort were Altamaha, Pocasabo, Chasee, Oketee, and Tulafina (Beaufort and Jasper Counties). The nation fled to Florida in 1715, during the Yamassee War, where they again received Spanish protection and continued to raid the South Carolina, and later Georgia, frontier until the 1740's.

YUCHI TOWN Indians of the Uchean stock consisting of about thirty men located near present North Augusta (Aiken County). A band of Chickasaw, a very warlike people, established a nearby sentry-town in 1723.

JACKSON'S FORT A fortification on John Jackson's plantation called Pon Pon located near present Jacksonborough (Colleton County). During the Yamassee War the garrison protected Pon Pon Bridge, spanning the Edisto River. However, the fort was foolishly abandoned. A large war party of Apalachee Indians and their allies from near present Augusta, Georgia, crossed the bridge undiscovered in July 1715, devastated the settlements between the Edisto and Stono rivers for a week, and burned Pon Pon Bridge during their withdrawal.

FORT JOHNSON The necessity for a fort to guard the main entrance to Charles Town harbor was demonstrated during the unsuccessful Spanish attack of October 1706 against the town. In 1708 Fort Johnson was constructed at

Windmill Point on the east end of James Island where a lookout, or watchhouse, had been established as early as 1685 (Charleston County). The fort was triangular shaped with three bastions, a battery guarding the harbor entrance, and a ravelin in front of the gateway. The walls were constructed of alternating layers of mud, pine saplings, and oyster shells. A palisade was planted in the moat. South Carolina soldiers garrisoned the fort throughout the colonial period. Captain James Sutherland was appointed to command Fort Johnson in 1722. When the South Carolina Council removed him from command in 1729 he petitioned the King of England for a royal commission to command the fort. Having connections, he received his commission in 1730 and resumed command of the fort the following year. However, in early 1737 the South Carolina government again removed him from his command despite his royal commission. A Commons House investigating committee had found the fort and its equipment dilapidated, the soldiers ill equipped or absent, and Sutherland's two-year-old son on the muster role as a soldier. Because of his royal commission the government was forced to reinstate him with back pay in 1739, but he died the following year. Subsequent commanders continued to receive a King's commission. Fort Johnson was South Carolina's oldest and most important colonial fort. Wind and waves seem to have washed away much of the original fort site.

FORT KING GEORGE During August 1720 Colonel John Barnwell, a South Carolina planter and soldier, met with the British Board of Trade in London and outlined his proposal for checking French expansion by building and garri-

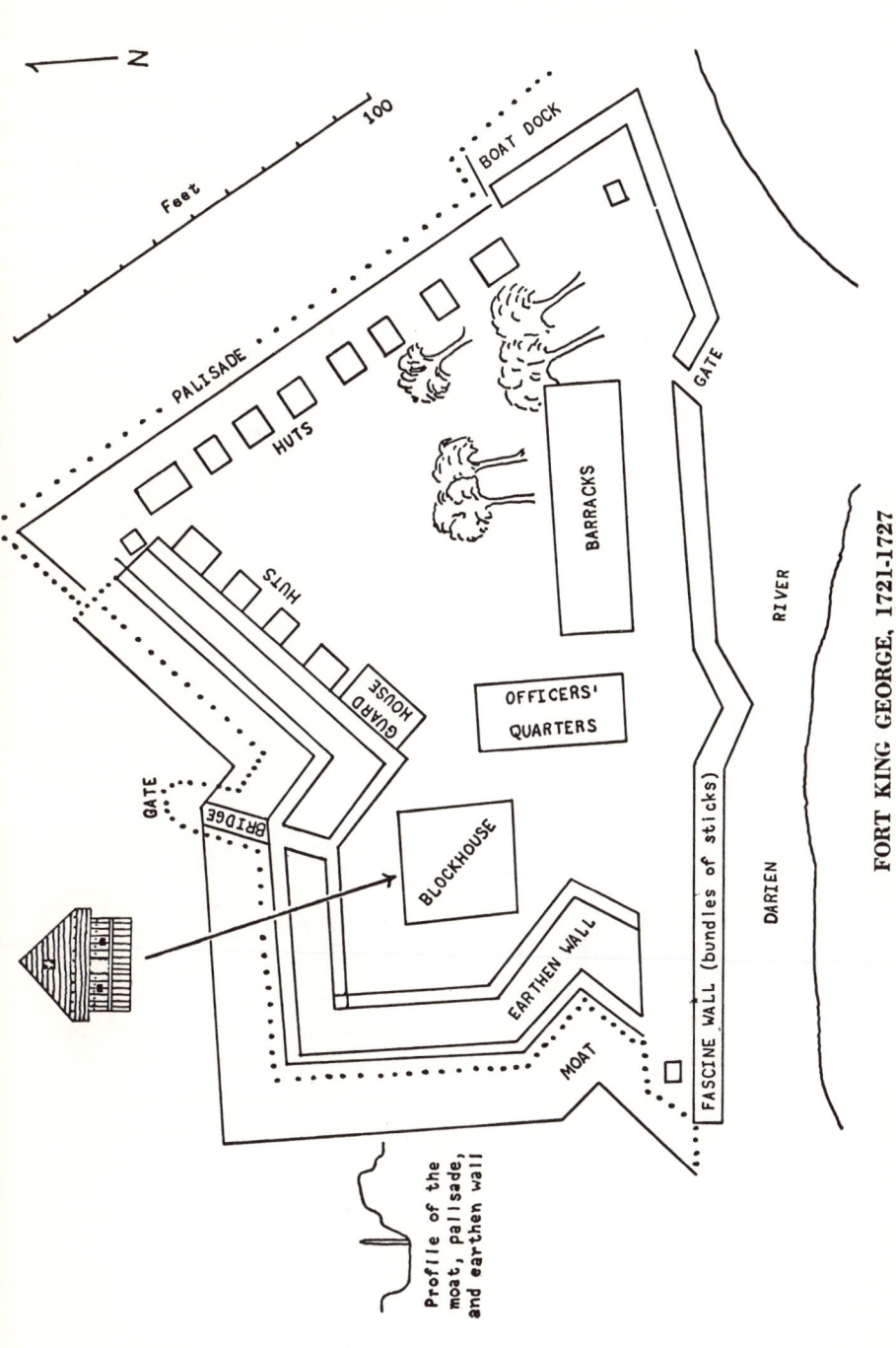

FORT KING GEORGE, 1721-1727. Courtesy of the British Public Record Office, London. A modified tracing of John Barnwell's plan of about 1722.

soning a number of forts beyond the frontier. He explained that the most urgent need was to construct a fort at the mouth of the Altamaha River in present Georgia in order to protect the southern frontier and deny that uninhabited, strategic area to both France and Spain. The Board approved Barnwell's plan and raised the Independent Company of Foot, a regular unit composed of old men and invalids, to garrison the proposed Altamaha fort. When Barnwell and the Independent Company arrived in South Carolina in 1721, the regulars were too sick to construct the fort. Instead, Barnwell took the scout boat crews from Beaufort and Passage forts and rowed to the Altamaha River where they began constructing Fort King George. The fort, located one mile southeast of present Darien, Georgia (McIntosh County, Georgia), was actually a redoubt. The main fortification was a strong, plank-sided blockhouse with a protruding third floor. The outworks consisted of an earthen wall (one side had only a palisade) in the shape of an irregular triangle, a moat, and a palisade planted in the moat. Fort King George was supposed to have been a temporary fortification until a regular fort could be built on St. Simons Island to the south-southeast. By 1722 most of the Independent Company was stationed there. It was a lonely, unhealthy site with no entertainment or diversions. During the six years the fort was garrisoned over one hundred and forty British regulars died of sickness, and many others deserted. The blockhouse and barracks burned in January 1726, and temporary barracks were constructed. However, in September 1727, when Yamassee war parties began a series of attacks against the frontier, Fort King

George was abandoned and the Independent Company was withdrawn to Beaufort Fort to protect South Carolina's southern settlements. A two-man lookout was maintained at Fort King George until 1734. Today the site is a Georgia state park and is being developed by the Georgia Historical Commission.

LAROCHE'S BRIDGE FORT   A fort constructed during the Yamassee War to guard the bridge (named for the nearby planter, James LaRoche) connecting Wadmalaw and Johns islands. The fort's location was evidently nine and one-half miles southwest of Charles Town on Johns Island, a short distance northwest of the bridge which crosses the heads of Church and Bohicket creeks (Charleston County). It contained an army garrison from August 1715 to March 1716.

LEE'S FORT   A private frontier fort during the Cherokee War of 1760-1761 located at the head of the east fork of Little River, about seven miles south of present Chester (Chester County).

LONG CANES FORT   The first major Indian depredation of the Cherokee War was inflicted against the settlers living near Long Canes Creek, forty miles northwest of Augusta. When Cherokee war parties began descending upon the settlements, the settlers at Long Canes packed their possessions and began a flight to Augusta, Georgia. A large war party attacked the wagon train as it was crossing Long Canes Creek on February 1, 1760. More than fifty settlers, mostly women and children, were killed or captured. Later that year some of the settlers returned to Long Canes, and under the protection of a party of friendly Chickasaw

Indians they built a stockade fort on the east side of Long Canes Creek probably about five miles northwest of present McCormick (McCormick County). Another fortification named Fort Adventure may have been built nearby on the Savannah River.

LOOKOUTS (WATCH HOUSES) Coastal South Carolina was extremely vulnerable to waterborne raids by Indians and Spaniards. An Indian raiding party in canoes could approach any of the principal settlements and plantations from Florida by way of the intracoastal waterway. Lone privateers or small fleets of Spanish ships could easily conduct surprise attacks from the Atlantic Ocean. The best means of combating these sudden raids was to receive an early warning of the appearance of raiding canoes or ships and then muster the militia to oppose them. In order to receive early warning it was necessary to place men along the coast to maintain a constant watch. In 1685, with the beginning of serious trouble with the Spaniards in Florida, watchmen, later called lookouts, were stationed near the entrance to Charles Town harbor. By Queen Anne's War (1701-1713) lookouts were stationed from Daufuskie Island in the south to Bull Island in the north. Lookouts were maintained during times of crisis until France and Spain surrendered their possessions in eastern North America in 1763. Lookouts were established at various times on the following islands (present names are used): Daufuskie, Hilton Head, Bay Point (south end of St. Helena), St. Helena, Otter, Edisto, James, Sullivans, Long, and Bull. A watch house was usually built at each lookout site to house the men. It was constructed of a pole frame, sided with rough clapboards. A small, crude observation tower stood nearby. They were usually issued cannons which were used to signal the presence of a hostile party. Those without cannons used beacon fires as a signalling device. Most lookout stations were provided with dugout canoes to use in patrolling and for escape in the event of hostile approach. The scout boat system was an outgrowth of the "scout watch," lookouts who also patrolled in canoes.

FORT LOUDOUN The building of this fort among the Overhill Towns, the most remote of the Cherokee Nations, was an ill advised, impractical venture. Its garrison was supposed to protect the Overhill Cherokees who were dangerously exposed to the French and their Indian allies, and to prevent the Overhill warriors from murdering their English traders and joining the French of their own accord. Its remoteness, three hundred and fifty miles from Charles Town across the Great Smoky Mountains, rendered it impossible to reinforce or resupply without the Cherokees' cooperation. William De Brahm, an engineer, began building the fort in 1757 on the southwest bank of Little Tennessee River near present Vonore, Tennessee, twenty-nine miles southwest of Knoxville (Monroe County, Tennessee). Captain Raymond Demere finished the construction and commanded the garrison of British regular soldiers. The fort was diamond shaped with a bastion at each corner. A moat was dug and a crude earthen wall was packed against the outside of a palisade. Inside were erected a commander's house, barracks, a magazine, a blacksmith shop, and a guardhouse. Relations between the Cherokees on the one hand and their traders and the frontier settlers on the other continually worsened until, in 1759, the Cherokees began conducting raids against the frontier settlements. The fort's new commander, Captain Paul Demere (Raymond's brother) prepared for the coming war by butchering and salting the fort's herd of cattle and picking the corn which the garrison had planted. Full war began in January 1760, and the Cherokees drew a siege around Fort Loudoun. For the next seven months the British soldiers and a few traders lived inside the fort's walls. Each man was reduced to eating a pint of corn per day. Despite the tightness of the siege several of the soldiers' Cherokee mistresses continued to visit the fort with small amounts of food. Captain Demere managed to ransom a few civilians which ranging war parties had taken on the frontier. The fort's heroes were the men who carried messages through the Indian lines. Abraham, a Negro slave, bravely evaded the Cherokee warriors on two occasions to carry messages to the South Carolina government. He unselfishly undertook the second trip to and from the fort after being rewarded with his freedom for the first journey. During the summer a large relief expedition consisting of British regulars and South Carolina provincials failed to reach the fort. In August, after the garrison had eaten everything including the traders' horses, Captain Demere surrendered to the Cherokees. The Indians were to take possession of Fort Loudoun and its armament and care for the sick soldiers. The garrison was to be allowed to march unharmed to Fort Prince George. During the second day of the garrison's withdrawal the Cherokees disregarded their promise and attacked. About thirty men and women were killed, and the remainder

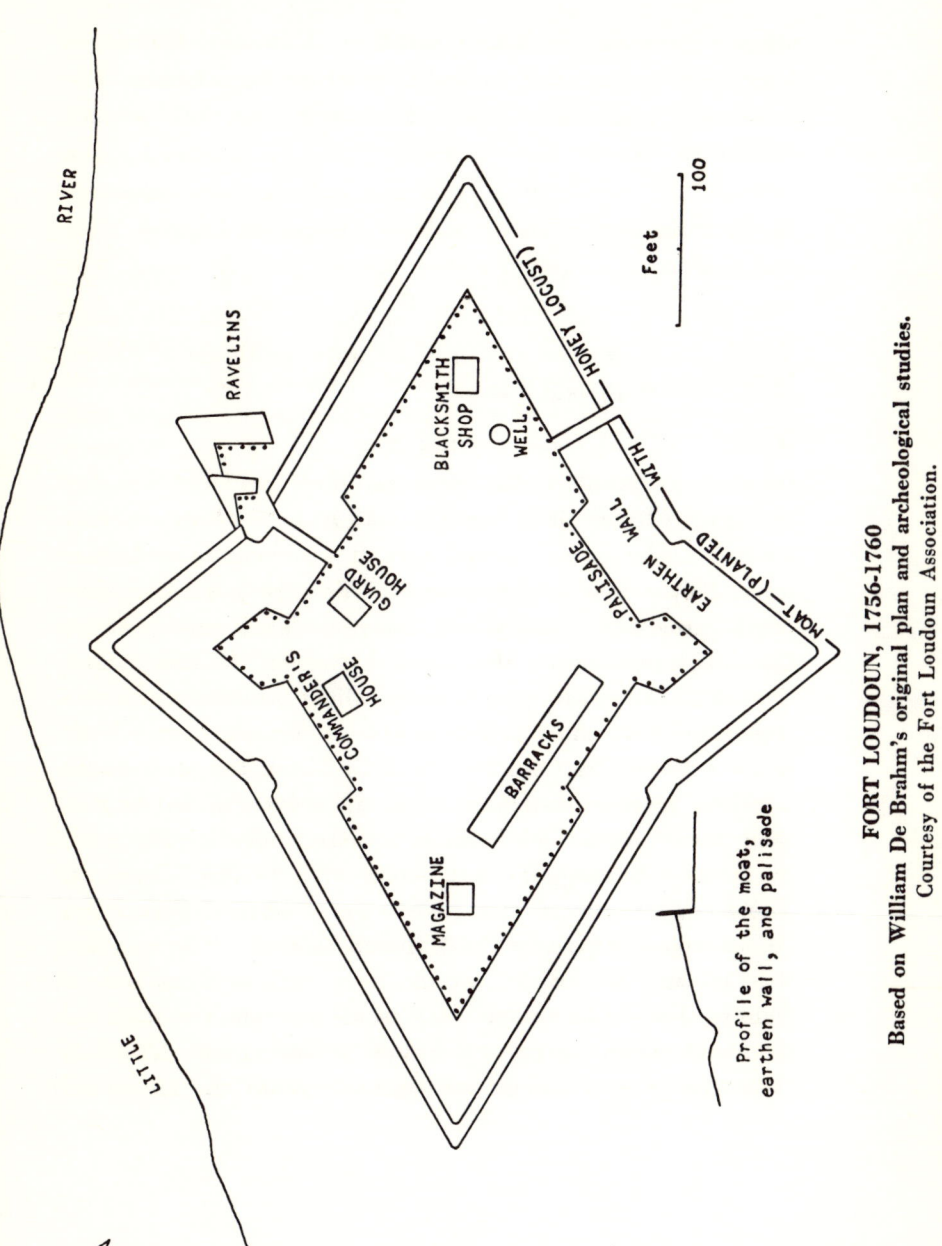

FORT LOUDOUN, 1756-1760
Based on William De Brahm's original plan and archeological studies.
Courtesy of the Fort Loudoun Association.

of the garrison was taken prisoner. Captain Demere was captured and tortured to death. Most of the prisoners were eventually ransomed. The Indians destroyed the fort soon afterward. Today Fort Loudoun has been partially reconstructed and serves as a Tennessee historical site under the supervision of the Fort Loudoun Association.

LYLES' FORT A private frontier fort built during the Cherokee War of 1760-1761 on the east side of Beaver Creek about thirteen and one-half miles southeast of present Whitmire (Fairfield County).

FORT LYTTELTON During the 1740's there were constant reports made to the South Carolina Assembly that Fort Prince Frederick near Beaufort had to be repaired or, preferably, replaced with a new fort. It wasn't until 1758, however, that a new fort was begun. For the next four years work progressed slowly on the new fortification, named Fort Lyttelton after the royal Governor William Henry Lyttelton. It was located in an excellent position on Spanish Point, a mile and a half south of Beaufort across the harbor (Beaufort County). Stuart's Town, the seventeenth-century Scottish settlement, and apparently Beaufort Fort had been previously established there. Fort Lyttelton was built in the shape of a triangle four hundred by three hundred seventy-five feet with the base on Port Royal River and the point on the inland side. The point was a bastion and the corners at the base were half-bastions. A tabby (lime and oyster shell cement) retainer wall was constructed, and a moat was dug outside on the land side. The dirt from the moat was packed against the tabby wall as an additional protection from cannon balls and shot. It is unknown if a palisade was planted around the fort. On the river side the tabby wall was perforated with embrasures for cannons which rested on a plank platform eighteen feet

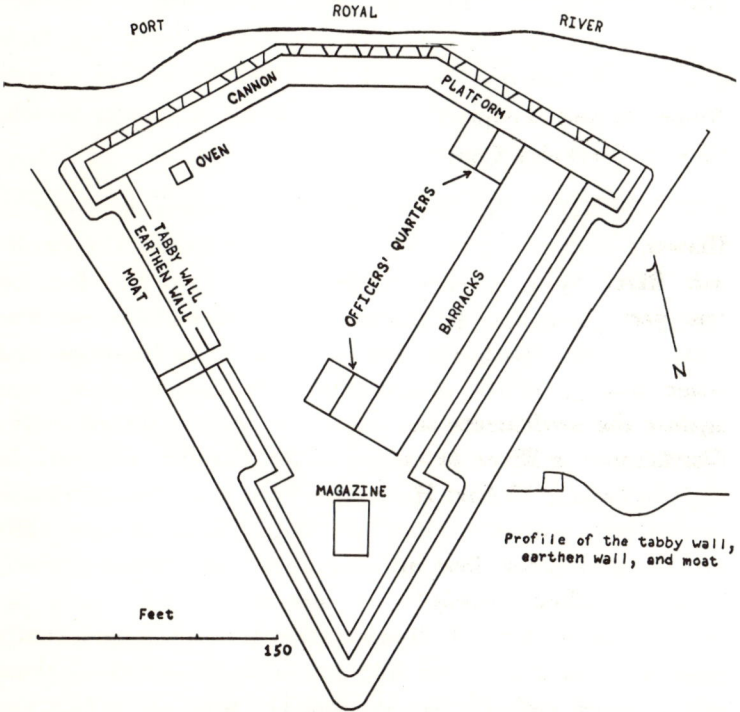

FORT LYTTELTON, 1758-1775
Based on a 1775 plan in the *South Carolina Historical and Genealogical Magazine*, II (Jan., 1901), and period descriptions.

wide. Small officers' houses, a large barracks building, a magazine, a well, latrines, and an oven were constructed inside. A gunner and a handful of South Carolina soldiers garrisoned the fort until at least 1766. British regulars may have served as an addition to the garrison from time to time. Today only the outline of a portion of the moat and fallen portions of the tabby wall are visible.

MEPKIN FORT A fortified house on Sir Peter Colleton's Mepkin plantation during the Westo War of 1680. The location was on the east bank of the West Branch of Cooper River, six and one-quarter miles southeast of present Moncks Corner (Berkeley County).

FORT MOORE In the early 1700's Savannah Town, a Shawnee Indian sentry-town, was located across the Savannah River from present Augusta, Georgia. The location was very strategic; it protected the major northwestern entrance into South Carolina. In 1715 the Shawnee and other nearby tribes joined the Yamassee in their war against the settlements and soon fled southwestward to the Chattahoochee River to escape South Carolina reprisal. In the winter of 1715 Fort Moore was built near the abandoned Indian town atop a two hundred foot bluff on the east bank of Savannah River, four miles southeast of present Augusta, Georgia (Aiken County). Its construction was under the supervision of Gerard Monger, the garrison's commander from 1716 to 1725. The fort was a large structure, about one hundred and fifty feet square. The wall, about four and one-half feet high, was constructed of planks which were nailed to upright posts. In 1747 the wall was built higher and a platform walkway was constructed around the inside. There were no earthworks and no moat. Cannons were mounted in bastions at each corner, and each bastion was covered by a shed. Inside the fort were officers' houses, barracks, a guardhouse, a magazine, traders' storehouses, a corn crib, and other buildings. A unit of South Carolina provincials, varying between ten and forty men, garrisoned the fort until 1746. British soldiers were stationed there intermittently from 1746 to 1766 when it was abandoned after fifty years of service. The nearby settlement of Savannah Town, later called New Windsor, served as the headquarters for the Creek Indian traders until the 1740's when the Georgia settlement of Augusta assumed that role. The hard drinking traders with their illiterate packhorsemen, Indian wives, and halfbreed children created continuous problems for captains like Daniel Pepper who commanded from 1737 to 1745. Fort Moore was the most important of South Carolina's early frontier forts.

MULBERRY FORT A private fortified house on Thomas Broughton's plantation named Mulberry located on the west bank of Cooper River, three and one-half miles south-southeast of present Moncks Corner (Berkeley County). Refugees from the surrounding countryside fled to Broughton's plantation and remained there during much of the Yamassee War of 1715-1716. It is believed by some that the present mansion, Mulberry Castle, was the same house which served as the Yamassee War fortification.

MURRAY'S FORT A private frontier fort constructed on Dr. John Murray's plantation located on Hard Labor Creek. The exact location is unknown, but it was probably about ten miles south of present Greenwood (Greenwood County). It was built in early 1764 during Creek Indian raids against the Long Canes settlements. At one time about one hundred and fifty people were housed there.

FORT NINETY SIX (FORT MIDDLETON) The area around Ninety Six Creek received its name from Cherokee traders in the early 1700's because it was ninety-six trail miles from there to Keowee in the Cherokees' Lower Towns where Fort Prince George was constructed in 1753. Traders' storehouses were maintained at Ninety Six for several years. During the middle of the eighteenth century that area of the frontier, the country around Saluda River, contained a number of South Carolinians who, like the Indians, made their living by hunting deer and selling the skins. These illiterate, hardy men became expert woodsmen, sometimes surpassing Indian warriors in the techniques of forest warfare. They were often recruited as valuable members of ranger troops which were raised during times of Indian trouble. During the 1750's settlers began moving into the Ninety Six area to establish farms. For many years the principal settler was James Francis, a militia commander and a captain of provincial rangers during 1748 and 1755. With the beginnings of trouble with the Cherokees in 1759 the Ninety Six settlement, astride the path leading from the Cherokee Nations into the settled areas, became a strategic position. Governor William Henry Lyttelton arrived there in November 1759 with a militia army which was supposed to overawe the Cherokees. Before marching on to Fort Prince George at Keowee Town the governor constructed Fort Ninety Six, a small, square stockade built around Robert Goudey's barn located ten miles southeast of present Greenwood (Greenwood County). On February 3, 1760, after Lyttelton's force had withdrawn from the frontier, a Cherokee war party appeared before the fort. After finding the fort too strong to attack, the Indians fired from a distance and then withdrew. A month later the fort was again attacked, and again the garrison of settlers under the command of James Francis beat off the war party. Until April 1761 the fort's militia soldiers served as a provincial garrison. By May of that year a new stockade had been constructed around the fort. Thomas Bell assumed command of the fort toward the end of the war.

NIXON'S FORT   A private frontier fort during the Cherokee War of 1760-1761. It was located on Edward Nixon's land somewhere on the east side of Little River, west or southwest of present Winnsboro (Fairfield County).

OTTERSON'S FORT   A private frontier fort probably built on James Otterson's land during the Cherokee War of 1760-1761. The exact location is unknown, but it was apparently on the west side of Tyger River, south or southwest of present Union (Union County).

PASSAGE FORT   In December 1717 one of the two scout boats at Beaufort Fort was ordered stationed further south on the Inland Passage, present Intracoastal Waterway. The location of the Passage Fort was at Bloody Point on Daufuskie Island where a lookout appears to have been established in 1701, and the site where a scout boat force had defeated a large party of Yamassees in the summer of 1715 (Beaufort County). The site was intermittently garrisoned by scouts until the scout boat service was discontinued in 1764. Early in 1728 a Yamassee war party surprised the garrison and killed or captured everyone. Passage Fort was probably a crude structure consisting of a large clapboard hut surrounded by a palisade of logs. Other nearby sites which also served as occasional scout boat bases were Calibogue Point (present Braddock Point on Hilton Head Island) and St. Phillips Point on present Bay Point Island.

PATTON'S FORT   A private frontier fort built on Arthur Patton's land during the early part of 1764 when Creek Indians were raiding the Long Canes settlements. It was located on Little River near present Calhoun Falls (Abbeville or McCormick County). For a time during 1764 the fort contained one hundred and thirty-nine refugees.

PEARSON'S FORT   A private frontier fort built on land owned by John Pearson during the Cherokee War of 1760-1761. The location was on the west side of Broad River, about twelve miles northwest of present Columbia (Richland County).

PENNINGTON'S FORT   A private frontier fort during the Cherokee War of 1760-1761 built on Jacob Pennington's land located on the south side of Indian Creek, six miles south of present Whitmire (Newberry County).

PONDS FORT   A fortified house during the Yamassee War of 1715-1716. It was located on Andrew Percival's plantation called The Ponds and Western (or Weston) Hall, six miles southwest of present Summerville on the east side of Ashley River (Dorchester County). It was probably a local militia garrison from April to August 1715. An army unit garrisoned the fort during the period August 1715 to March

1716. This was the staging point for the army which marched to the Cherokee Nations in November 1715 during the latter stages of the war.

FORT PRINCE FREDERICK This fort was slowly built during the period 1731 to 1734 as a replacement for Beaufort Fort. The site was the same as that of the present U. S. Navy Hospital three miles south of Beaufort. It was a small fort one hundred twenty-five by seventy-five feet with tabby walls about five feet thick and four feet high on three sides. One bastion was built on the southwest side. Along the eastern wall was a battery of cannons commanding Port Royal River. A moat with a palisade planted in the bottom may have surrounded the land side, and earth may have been packed against the outside of the tabby wall. Barracks crowded the inside along with a magazine. The garrison varied from two provincials to one hundred British regulars. The Independent Company of Foot, a unit of British regulars, garrisoned the fort until they were transferred to Georgia in 1736. During the next two years provincial soldiers were stationed there. British soldiers from the 42nd Regiment in Georgia provided a garrison from 1738 until about 1744. Regulars of a newly raised Independent Company began garrisoning the fort in 1746, and British soldiers continued to be stationed there intermittently until a new fortification, Fort Lyttelton, was begun in 1758. Provincial scout boats were also stationed at the fort periodically throughout its existence. Fort Prince Frederick was built in a very poor location militarily. High ground commanded the fort on the west side and Port Royal River virtually touched the eastern wall. The morale of the

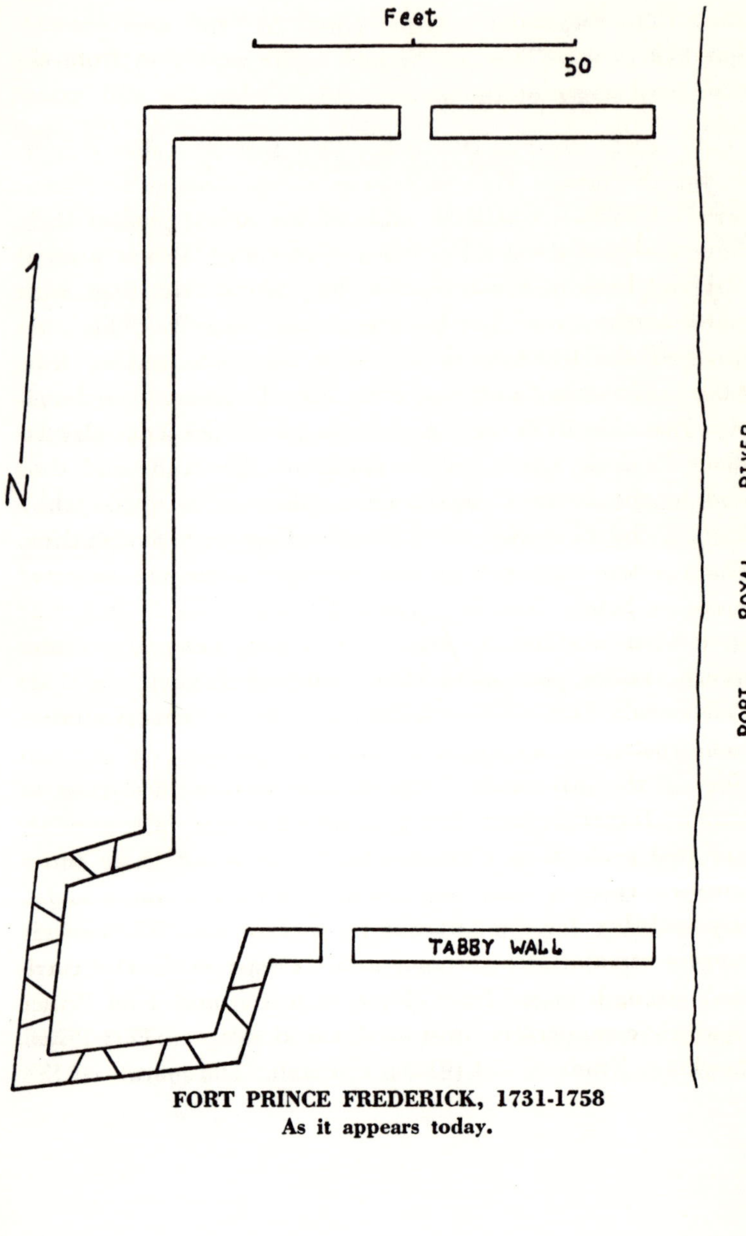

FORT PRINCE FREDERICK, 1731-1758
As it appears today.

soldiers in the garrison appears to have been at a constant low ebb. During the 1730's and 1740's desertion from the fort reached epidemic proportions. Today the still extant tabby walls of the fort are well maintained by the staff of the U. S. Navy Hospital, Beaufort.

FORT PRINCE GEORGE (PALACHACOLA) Palachacola, or Apalachicola, was a Hitchiti Indian sentry-town located on the west bank of the Savannah River about thirty-five miles north-northwest of present Savannah, Georgia. The town guarded the strategic point where the trail leading from Charles Town to Saint Augustine, Florida, crossed the Savannah River. In 1715 the Palachacola joined the Yamassee Indians in their attack on the frontier settlements, and then fled to the lower Chattahoochee River to escape reprisal. During the first half of 1718 the Company of Southern Rangers was stationed across the river from the deserted town in South Carolina. From 1719 to 1721 a fort may have been established there as a trading factory, a center where trading was conducted with the Indians. In 1723 Palachacola Fort, or Fort Prince George (its formal name), was constructed by Captain William Bellinger on the east side of the Savannah River in the northwest corner of present Jasper County. The outworks consisted of a palisade wall and perhaps an earthen wall. It was occupied by South Carolina rangers until the new colony of Georgia assumed responsibility for the fort and its garrison in 1735. Georgia rangers remained in garrison until at least 1742. The garrison's strength varied from eleven to thirty men. Fort Prince George's commanders were William Bellinger (1723-1724), Rowland Evans (1724-1732), Philemon Parmenter (1732-

1734), Aneas Mackintosh, heir to the chieftainship of Clan Mackintosh in Scotland (1734-1740), and John Mackintosh (1740-1742).

FORT PRINCE GEORGE (KEOWEE) The South Carolina Assembly considered building a fort among the Cherokee Nations as early as 1729 to guard the northern entrance into the colony, to help protect the Cherokees from attacks by Indian allies of France, and to protect the South Carolina traders from insults by the Cherokees. Recommendations for a fort continued to be made until 1753 when the aggressive Governor James Glen personally led an expedition into the Lower Towns and constructed Fort Prince George. The fort was located on the east bank of Keowee River near the Cherokee town of Keowee, eleven miles south-southwest of present Pickens (Pickens County). It was one hundred feet square, having earthen walls with a palisade on top and a bastion at each corner. Inside were a commander's house, a barracks, a barracks-storehouse, a kitchen, a magazine, and a guardhouse. It was completely rebuilt in 1756 and again in 1765. A detachment from one of the three British Independent Companies stationed in South Carolina served as its garrison until 1764, and a garrison from the British Royal American Regiment was maintained there until about 1766. During the Cherokee War of 1760-1761 the garrison, under the command of Lieutenant Richard Coytmore, lived under siege for five months. The siege began in January 1760 when Lieutenant Coytmore frustrated a Cherokee plot to destroy the garrison by sending a party of warriors inside under the pretext of peace. During February 1760 the Cherokees managed to ambush

South Carolina, 1670–1775

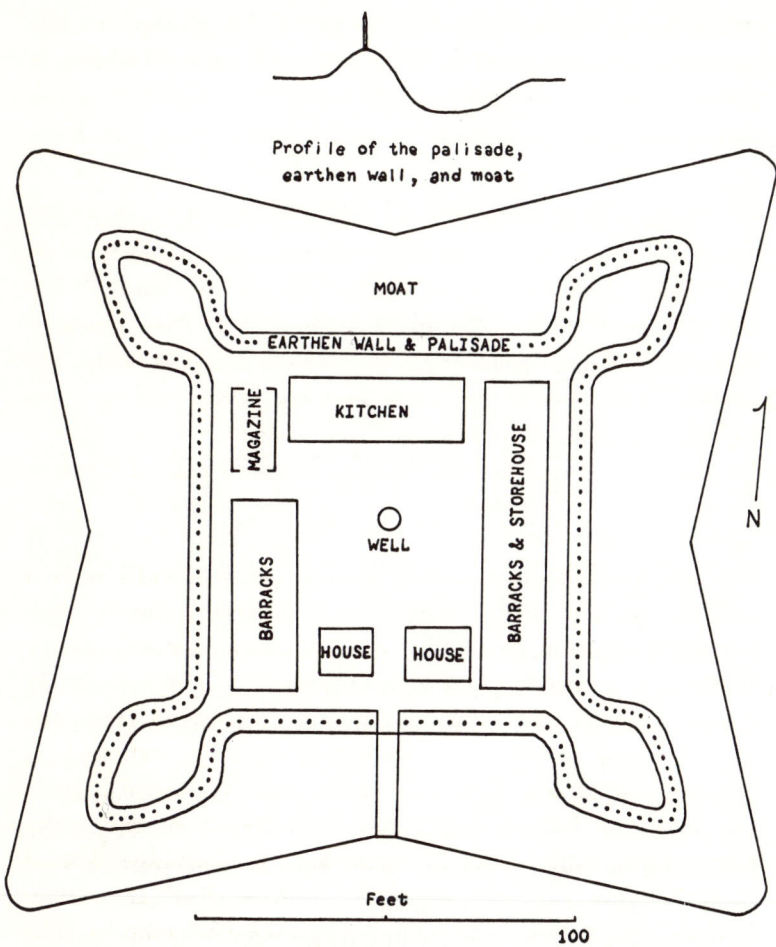

FORT PRINCE GEORGE (KEOWEE), 1753-1768
Based on archeological studies by John D. Combes.
Courtesy of the Institute of Archeology and Anthropology,
University of South Carolina

and kill Coytmore whom they hated. The soldiers in the garrison, furious because of Coytmore's death, killed a number of Cherokees who were being held hostage in the fort. During the siege more of the garrison were lost from smallpox than Cherokee bullets. In June a large force of British and provincial soldiers reached the fort and raised the siege after marching from Charles Town. During the period 1966-1968 John D. Combes of the University of South Carolina conducted a complete archeological excavation of the fort. A Fort Prince George Museum is planned for the future. Today the site is under Keowee Lake.

RAIFORD'S FORT   A private frontier fort built on Philip Raiford's land during the Cherokee War of 1760-1761. It was located on the east side of Little River, about fifteen miles north-northwest of present Columbia (Fairfield County).

RICHBOURG'S FORT   The fortified house of Claude de Richbourg located on the west side of Santee River, about twenty and one-half miles east-northeast of present Moncks Corner (Berkeley County). Reverend Claude de Richbourg was the Huguenot rector of St. James Santee Parish, a settlement of French protestants. On May 6, 1715, at the beginning of the Yamassee War, the French settlers fled from their exposed plantations, but they returned a week later and made a fort of Richbourg's house. The fort served as a militia and an army garrison until about March 1716.

ST. GILES FORT   A fortified house during the Westo War of 1680 on Lord Ashley's St. Giles Kusso plantation located about five miles south-southwest of present Summerville (Dorchester County).

SALTCATCHERS FORT Between the years 1728 and 1731 Captain James McPherson and his Company of Southern Rangers built this stockade fort on the west side of Salkehatchie River, then called Saltcatchers, about three quarters of a mile east of present Yamassee (Beaufort County). The rangers were to patrol the area between Combahee River and Savannah River, protecting the Beaufort settlers from raids by Yamassee war parties. In early 1733 Captain McPherson and most of his company were sent to protect the new colony of Georgia. Lieutenant Aneas Mackintosh and a detachment of rangers from Fort Prince George (Palachacola) reinforced the men left behind. In 1734 Saltcatchers Fort was destroyed, and its garrison of rangers was moved to Fort Prince George.

SCHENCKINGH'S FORT A fort established in May 1715, during the Yamassee War, on the cowpen (cattle ranch) owned by Benjamin Schenckingh located on the south bank of the Santee River, twenty miles northwest of present Moncks Corner (Berkeley County). During June 1715 a war party of Catawba Indians and their allies attacked the fort and its thirty-man army garrison. Under the pretext of conducting negotiations the war party gained entrance, killed or captured all but a few of the defenders, and burned the fort. Today the site is covered by Lake Marion.

STEVENS CREEK FORT The Stevens Creek settlements were located northwest of Augusta near the Savannah River. At the beginning of the Cherokee War, in February 1760, the settlers began fleeing to Augusta to escape advancing war parties. During their flight a Cherokee war party caught up with them and killed a large number. Some of the settlers evidently returned in April and constructed Stevens Creek Fort between Savannah River and Stevens Creek, southeast of present McCormick (McCormick County).

STONO BRIDGE FORT A Yamassee War fort built on John Beamer's plantation to protect the bridge crossing Stono River to Johns Island, eleven miles west of Charles Town (Charleston County). An Army unit was garrisoned there from August 1715 to March 1716.

TOBLER'S FORT A private frontier fort built on John Tobler's plantation during the Cherokee War of 1760-1761. The site was on the east bank of Savannah River, five miles southeast of Augusta (Aiken County). Tobler, a Swiss immigrant, was the author of *The South-Carolina Almanack* which was published during most of the years from 1750 to 1765. At the beginning of the Cherokee War, in February 1760, a Cherokee war party passed through the area causing minor damage. The fort was built shortly afterward.

TURNER'S FORT A private frontier fort built during the Cherokee War of 1760-1761 on William Turner's plantation located north of present Batesburg on the south side of the confluence of Saluda and Little Saluda rivers (Saluda County). When the settlers living along the lower Saluda River began building Turner's fort in February 1760 they were attacked by a Cherokee war party. After four hours of fighting the militia under Captain Andrew Brown drove the Indians away, having killed several.

WAGGENER'S FORT A private frontier fort built on John Waggener's land during the Cherokee War of 1760-1761. Its location was on the east side of Beaver Creek thirteen miles west of present Whitmire (Fairfield County).

WANTOOT FORT A fortified house during the Yamassee War on the plantation owned by Pierre de St. Julian (afteward owned by the Ravenel family) located seven and a half miles north of present Moncks Corner (Berkeley County). Local militia were probably stationed there during the period April to August 1715. From August 1715 to March 1716 the garrison consisted of North Carolina soldiers, and the fort was the headquarters of the Northward Regiment. Today the site is under Lake Moultrie.

WASSAMASSAW FORT A Yamassee War fortification constructed on Ralph Izard's cowpen located six miles northwest of present Summerville (Dorchester County). The cowpen was also called Clear Spring and The Cypress. An army unit was in garrison there from May to August 1715. Local militia soldiers were probably stationed in the fort during the period August 1715 to about March 1716.

FORT WILLIAM HENRY LYTTELTON (MUSGROVE'S FORT) A private frontier fort constructed during the Cherokee War of 1760-1761. It was located on the west side of Enoree River about six and one-half miles southeast of present Whitmire (Newberry County). The fort's commander was Captain Edward Musgrove.

WILLTOWN FORT A fort built during the Yamassee War to protect the small village called Willtown, or New London, located on the east bank of Edisto River, twenty-eight and one-half miles southwest of Charles Town (Charleston County). It contained a militia garrison from April to August 1715. A large war party of Apalachee Indians and their allies from near present Augusta, Georgia, attacked the fort in July 1715, but were beaten off. During the period August 1715 to March 1716 the fort was used as a base for the province's scout boats.

WINYAH FORT This was a Yamassee War fortification which appears to have contained a small militia garrison under the command of Robert Screven during 1715. It was apparently located on the south side of Black River north-northwest of present Georgetown (Georgetown County).

WOFFORD'S FORT A private frontier fort during the Cherokee War of 1760-1761 which was probably located on the east side of Fair Forest Creek west of present Union (Union County).

WOODWARD'S FORT A fortification built in April 1715, during the Yamassee War, on John Woodward's plantation located on the west side of the head of Ashepoo River, eight and one-half miles south of present Walterboro (Colleton County). The fort guarded the major southern trail leading from Charles Town to Palachacola on the Savannah River. It was occupied by militia soldiers until March 1716 when an army garrison was established there. The Southern Rangers (Southward Division of Rangers), about thirty horsemen, were stationed there from December 1716 until December 1717 when they were moved to Palachacola.

Bibliography

Brown, Douglas S. *The Catawba Indians, The People of the River*. Columbia: University of South Carolina Press, 1966.

Corkran, David H. *The Cherokee Frontier, Conflict and Survival, 1740-62*. Norman: University of Oklahoma Press, 1962.

──────────. *The Creek Frontier, 1540-1783*. Norman: University of Oklahoma Press, 1967.

Crane, Verner W. *The Southern Frontier, 1670-1732*. Durham: Duke University Press, 1928; Ann Arbor: University of Michigan Press, 1956.

Meriwether, Robert L. *The Expansion of South Carolina, 1729-1765*. Kingsport: Southern, 1940.

Milling, Chapman J. *Red Carolinians*. Chapel Hill: University of North Carolina Press, 1940; Columbia: University of South Carolina Press, 1970.

Peterson, Harold L. *Forts in America*. New York: Scribner, 1964.